P9-CAN-599

What Did Jesus Do?

A Crash Course in His Life and Times

by
Michael L. Lindvall

Sterling Publishing Co., Inc.
New York

A John Boswell Associates Book

Text Design by Nan Jernigan

Library of Congress Cataloging-in-Publication Data available

2 4 6 8 10 9 7 5 3 1

Published by Sterling Publishing Co., Inc.
387 Park Avenue South, New York, NY 10016
© 2006 by Sterling Publsihing Co.

Distributed in Canada by Sterling Publishing
c/o Canadian Manda Group, 165 Dufferin Street
Toronto, Ontario, Canada M6K 3H6
Distributed in the United Kingdom by
GMC Distribution Services
Castle Place, 166 High Street, Lewes, East Sussex,
England BN7 1XU
Distributed in Australia by Capricorn Link (Australia) Pty. Ltd.
P.O. Box 704, Windsor, NSW 2756, Australia

Printed in China
All rights reserved

Sterling ISBN-13:978-1-4027-4088-6
        ISBN-10: 1-4027-4088-3

For information about custom editions, special sales, premium and
corporate purchases, please contact Sterling Special Sales
Department at 800-805-5489 or specialsales@sterlingpub.com.

Also by Michael L. Lindvall

The Good News from North Haven

Leaving North Haven

A Geography of God

To my wife, Terri,
and our children, Madeline,
Benjamin, and Grace

Acknowledgments

I would express my deep appreciation to all who read the manuscript for this book with sharp and faithful eyes and offered wisdom and insights that made it a better volume. I would thank Dr. Iain R. Torrance, friend and president of Princeton Theological Seminary, and Dr. C. Clifton Black, Otto A. Piper Professor of Biblical Theology at the same institution, for their corrections and superb suggestions. In fact, for readers of this book wishing to go deeper, I would commend the newly published *Anatomy of the New Testament* that Clifton has authored with Moody Smith and Robert Spivey. Any remaining oversights are, however, strictly mine. I would also thank friend and editor, John Boswell, who conceived this book, offered me the opportunity to write it, and worked with me to make it a more helpful book to a wide range of readers.

Table of Contents

AUTHOR'S NOTE

The Real Jesus, the Historical Jesus, and the Jesus of the Gospels

Nobody can ever know the whole "real" story of any historical figure. There's simply no way to discover all the minute details of any life, even one lived recently, much less one lived two thousand years ago. There's always more than we can know, and what we do know is invariably more complex, nuanced, and ambiguous than any historical writer or witness could ever perfectly record. So even though we know a lot about Jesus as ancient figures go, there is no earthly way of know everything. Jesus of Nazareth will always remain just beyond our full grasp.

In the last two centuries, biblical scholars have brought the academic disciplines of historical research to the study of scripture. They have worked to understand Jesus better by comparing the Gospels, those ancient stories of Jesus, carefully with each other, by investigating the world Jesus lived in, by studying other contemporary religious developments, and by sometimes looking at Christian documents that were not included in the New Testament. Some of these scholars have labored to draw a new picture of what they call the "historical" Jesus. In so doing, they have often come up with images of Jesus sharply different from the picture of Jesus the four Gospels of the New Testament present.

Though this quest for the historical Jesus has sometimes helped us understand Jesus more accurately, a few problems are obvious. First, besides the four Gospels, there is simply not much additional reliable information about him. Second, and most problematic, these scholars have come up with wildly different pictures of the historical Jesus. And, finally, in more than a few cases the historical Jesus that a scholar has produced has looked remarkably like the scholar himself.

So despite the contributions that the quest for the historical Jesus may have made, this book will unapologetically present Jesus as we meet him in the four Gospels of the New Testament. It will, however, make use of that historical research into Jesus and his times about which most Bible scholars agree and bring it cautiously to this overview. It is also important to remember that each of the four Gospels presents Jesus distinctively. There is simply no way to puree the four Gospels into one cream-soup story of Jesus' life. Nevertheless, this book will outline his life in a way that attends to each Gospel version of it without blending them into one story. Quotations from the Bible are drawn from the Revised Standard Version, though I have occasionally altered a word here and there to reflect newer scholarship. The ancient and present hope is that in viewing his singular life from those four different vantage points, and by looking through the lens of what we know about the world he lived in, we will be able to see Jesus more truly and better understand what he did.

IN THE MIDDLE OF NOWHERE

Sometime between the years 7 BC and 4 BC, a child was born in an obscure village in an obscure province at the eastern edge of the Roman Empire. ("Why not in year one?" you ask. We'll get to that puzzle in the next chapter.) His mother was a peasant girl, probably a young teenager. She was engaged to a man doubtless many years her senior; it seems they were not exactly formally wed when the baby came.

One of the sources of the story of his birth, the Gospel according to Luke, tells us that when the child was born the couple was away from home, the village of Nazareth in Galilee in the north of the country now called Israel. They had traveled more than sixty miles south through or around another region called Samaria to a small village named Bethlehem in the province of Judea, a daunting trip for a young girl nine months pregnant. They were on the road at this awkward time

1

because, Luke's Gospel tells us, a census was being taken and everybody had to go to their ancestral village to be counted. Joseph, young Mary's older husband-to-be, was a descendant of an ancient king of Israel, David, who had lived a thousand years earlier and had hailed from Bethlehem. Bethlehem may have been ancient, but it was no grand place, probably just a dot on the map five miles south of Jerusalem, that spiritual capital of the Jewish world and administrative capital of the Roman province of Judea.

There, in what was probably not much more than a wide spot in the road, Mary's first child was born. Luke tells us that the local inn was full, so perhaps Mary gave birth in the stable out back or maybe in a nearby cave, but most likely on the first floor of the inn where the innkeeper kept his sheep or cattle. Paying customers normally slept upstairs with other people. The child was probably born during the night. Mary named him Jesus (as we render it in English). It was a common enough name among good Jews at the time. It was a Hebrew name, even though the couple probably spoke Aramaic, the common language among local Jews in those days. Either way, it would have been pronounced "Yeshu." "Yeshu" was a shortened version of "Yeshua" which was itself an abbreviated form of "Yehoshua," or "Joshua" as we spell it in English. A good old-fashioned name for a good Jewish boy, "Joshua" had originally meant "God helps," but by the time Jesus was born, most people understood his name to mean "God saves." A very proper name, as time would tell.

Most people know the bare outline of the story I just

told you. They know it well enough that they look right past the irony woven into its details. How ironic that this child born in an obscure village, this child born to peasants, this child born on the ragged edge of legitimacy, this child born in the ancient equivalent of a barn, this child of perfectly routine, nobody special, middle-of-nowhere obscurity would grow into the man who would change history more than any other human being who ever lived. Jesus would never travel more than sixty miles from home, he would receive no known formal education, he would never write a book, he would probably never own more than the clothes on his back, he would die a shameful death, executed for sedition and blasphemy in his mid thirties. Yet two thousand years later, a third of the world's population would call themselves "Christians" after him, more adherents than any other religion or philosophy the world has ever known.

But if it's ironic that a life of such obscurity should have such an earth-shattering impact, there is a second, modern irony. This is the very irony that led to this little book: Jesus has influenced the world more than any other person who ever lived, so how ironic it is that most people today simply don't have a coherent grasp of precisely what he did in those thirty-five or so years. In our day, intelligent and literate people, non-Christians and Christians, often possess only the vaguest notions of this singular life that has so profoundly shaped our world.

Often, they know a story or two about Jesus. They've heard the Christmas story I just told. They've heard about the Sermon on the Mount with its list of Blessed are's . . . They may recall that Jesus told that parable called the Prodigal Son. They know about his death and resurrection, of course. But all these bits simply don't form themselves into a whole. They lie scattered randomly across the table of our modern minds. Smart and decently educated people, believers and skeptics alike, know individual stories about Jesus, stories often snatched out of context, but they've never had a chance to see the whole story of the life of Jesus in one big picture. More than a few people have worn those bracelets on their wrists with the abbreviation that asks, "WWJD?" "What would Jesus do?" Ironically, however, many don't know the answer to the question that lies behind the bracelet's inquiry: "WDJD?"—"What *did* Jesus do?"

This book offers a crash course on the life of Jesus. It begins with the assumption bright people often know rather little about Jesus, mostly bits and pieces. Of course, one could just read the Bible, especially the first four books of the second part of the Christian Bible, those four books called the Gospels. Perhaps this book will inspire some to do just that. The pages to follow are anything but another gospel, nor are they a biography of Jesus either. Rather, this book is simply aimed to help you shape a clear and cohesive picture of the life of Jesus and what he did.

To understand the life of Jesus—what he said and did and why he said it and did it—some background is essential. So fasten your seat belt for a drive-by of history. We'll pass a few of those landmarks you really need to see in order to understand the life of this man, born in such obscurity, who so changed the world.

WHEN AND WHERE

The modern world divides time in half. There is BC and AD, and the line down the middle, year one, is theoretically the year Jesus was born. BC stands for "before Christ" and AD stands for the Latin words, *anno Domini*, "in the year of the Lord." Lord Jesus Christ that is. The problem is . . . he wasn't born in year one.

In the ancient world there was no universal system for keeping track of the years. Usually, you just dated an event in relation to some other big event that everybody knew about, like the death of a king or the year some emperor came to the throne. Two of the four New Testament Gospels (Matthew and Luke) inform us in this fashion that Jesus was born during the reign of a Roman puppet-king of Judea named Herod the Great. We know from historical records that this Herod reigned between the years we now call 37 BC and 4 BC At the other end of Jesus' life, the Gospels tell us that

5

Jesus died during the tenure of a Roman governor of Judea named Pontius Pilate. Pilate was governor from AD 26 to AD 36. Finally, Luke's Gospel tells us that Jesus began his work of preaching and healing when "he was about thirty years old." And all four Gospels indicate that his ministry was fairly brief, probably just two or three years. So put all this together, and it means Jesus was probably born between 7 BC and 4 BC and died between about AD 30 and AD 33 when he was in his mid-thirties. His active years of ministry, the only years we know much about, probably fell between AD 27 and AD 33.

So why are all our calendars off by four to seven years? Why wasn't Jesus born in the year one? Well, nobody started counting the years from Jesus's birth (the "AD" idea) until the sixth century. All those years later when they sat down to figure out precisely how many years had passed since Jesus was born, they ended up a few years off in their computations.

But the real key to understanding is not so much precise dates as it is to know what Jesus' world was like between 7 BC and AD 33. What did people believe in? How did they think? What did they assume to be true? Who ran the political show? You really can't understand what Jesus did without some awareness of the way people lived, thought, and believed in his world. The answer to any particular "cultural-context question" would encompass three layers, because three major cultural and political realities were dominant in his time. First, there was the world of Greek culture and commerce. Second, there was the Roman Empire and, finally, there was the smaller but fascinating world of Jesus' native Judaism. The first two are important, but they don't matter nearly as much to understanding Jesus as the last one. And it matters a lot.

Those Greeks and the Romans

For many centuries before Jesus, the Greeks had been establishing colonies and building trade relationships around the Mediterranean. Greek culture, Greek philosophy, and the Greek language had become extremely influential, especially among the better educated and more sophisticated people of the Mediterranean world. The spread of Greek culture had been greatly enhanced by the military conquests of Alexander the Great who, some three centuries before Jesus, had conquered much of the world east of Greece. After his death, Alexander left several of his generals in control of most of his conquered real estate. The fashionable Greek culture that flourished around the central and eastern Mediterranean in the centuries during and after Alexander is usually called Hellenistic, meaning "Greek-like."

A version of Greek became the most common language of commerce and learning, and the usual means of communication among people who couldn't otherwise understand each other, especially in the eastern Mediterranean. This included Jesus' homeland. It was a simpler form of classical Greek called *Koine*. *Koine* simply means "common," as in the "common language of the streets." After Jesus' death, the Gospels that tell his story, indeed the entire Christian New

Testament, would be written in *Koine* Greek, not Aramaic, the language that Jesus and most other Jews in Judea and Galilee spoke, and not Hebrew, the ancient Jewish language, little-spoken by Jesus' time, but still the language in which most Jews read scripture in their synagogues.

This prominence of Greek language and culture made a difference to the story of Jesus in three important ways.

First, the four Gospels that tell Jesus' story would be written in Greek, and because of that, they would be understandable to diverse people across the ancient world. This "common" Greek language would be used to spread the story of Jesus, who was born and lived in such "common" circumstance, around the Mediterranean world in the first centuries after his life.

Second, Jesus would come into contact with Greek Gentiles a number of times in his life. "Gentile" was a term that Jews used for anybody who was not a Jew. Many, if not most of the Gentiles in Jesus' part of the world would probably have been Greek-speaking. Indeed, there was a string of Greek-speaking colonies just south and east of Jesus' native Galilee. Jesus would pay what was doubtless a controversial visit to this Greek Gentile region called the Decapolis, or "Ten Cities."

And third, even though Jesus' own thinking does not show much, if any, Greek influence, the Gospel writers would later use some Greek ideas when they told his story. For instance, the fourth Gospel, the Gospel of John, tells about Jesus coming into the world with these words: "The word became flesh, and dwelt among us." The Greek for "word" is in fact a venerable Greek philosophical term, *logos*. *Logos* had the weight of Greek thinking behind it, its ultimate source being the Greek philosopher Plato. The term meant everything from "speech" and "rational explanation," to "logic" or "creative power." It was surely not how Jesus would have talked about himself, but it became a way for some of his followers to talk about the meaning of his life, a way that was at least as Greek as it was Jewish.

The Roman World

When Alexander the Great died some three centuries before Jesus, he left his fragile empire in the hands of several of his generals and their political heirs. The next centuries were especially chaotic and brutal, even for the ancient world. Into this authority-vacuum, a new colonial power gradually edged its way toward world domination. Rome was a Latin-speaking city-state in central Italy famous (at first, at least) for austerity, discipline, and military prowess. In the century before Jesus, Roman power came to rule most of the Mediterranean world, including Jesus' homeland.

Earlier, about 175 years before Jesus, the Jews had wrestled power from one of Alexander's political heirs. They had briefly established an independent Jewish state under the leadership of a family named the Maccabees. But this short-lived Jewish independence ended in 63 BC when two Jewish rivals for power were foolish enough to ask the Romans for help. The Roman general Pompey "helped" by marching in and establishing a string of surrogate rulers under the Roman thumb. Herod the Great, who would sit on the throne when Jesus was born, was one of those Roman client-kings. In reality, of course, Caesar and his local governors, like the Pontius Pilot who would preside at Jesus' trial, held the real power.

Rome matters for the story of Jesus in at least two important ways.

First, it would be this Roman governor of Judea, Pontius Pilate, who would preside over Jesus's trial and death.

Second, the *Pax Romana*, or "Roman Peace," a heavy-handed period of relative stability and international law that Rome offered much of the Mediterranean world, would allow followers of Jesus, like the Apostle Paul, the opportunity to travel the known world and tell his story in a way that would have been much more difficult in an age of open warfare.

Jesus' Jewish World

Jesus was born a Palestinian Jew, lived his life as a Palestinian Jew, and died a Palestinian Jew. His followers addressed him as rabbi, a Jewish title that means "my teacher." He had an exceptional knowledge of the Jewish scriptures. One cannot understand Jesus without understanding the Jewish world he lived in.

Palestine and The Diaspora

During Jesus' lifetime, and in the centuries before and after, there were two groups of Jews. There were Jews who lived in Palestine, mostly in Judea and its capital,

Jerusalem, and Jews who lived in Galilee to the north, where Jesus was from. Galilee and Judea were separated by a region called Samaria, the homeland of the Samaritans, a religious and ethnic group related to Jews but generally despised as heretics. This, of course, is where the Good Samaritan of Jesus' famous parable was from. This region—Galilee, Samaria, and Judea—set at the eastern edge of the Mediterranean, was the ancestral homeland of the Jews. This larger area was then and has often since been referred to as "Palestine," a word that comes from the "Philistines," a people who had once settled along the coast. (David defeated the Philistine giant Goliath in the famous face-to-face battle.) Most of the Jews of Palestine spoke Aramaic, which was related to their ancient language, Hebrew, as well as to later Semitic languages like Arabic.

Then there were other Jews, thousands, perhaps even millions, who lived in Jewish communities outside Palestine around the Mediterranean basin and to the east at least as far as Persia. These were the Jews of the Diaspora, or "Dispersion." Most of these Diaspora Jews probably spoke koine Greek, Aramaic, some other local language, or even Latin. Generally, they were more influenced by the Hellenistic ideas flooding the world than were Jews back home in Palestine. Though Jesus belonged to the Palestinian group, these Diaspora Jews would play an important role in the spreading of his story. It would be among them, especially in their widely scattered urban synagogues, and among the non-Jews who often attended these Diaspora synagogues without formally converting to Judaism, that the story of Jesus would be told in the first decades after his death. In fact, Judaism, with its one God and rigorous moral claims, held a strong attraction for many Gentiles of the day, weary as they were of the old state religions of Greek and Roman paganism and the plethora of exotic local cults.

More Than One Way to Be Jewish

In Jesus' day, Judaism was a diverse and creative religion. In fact, it was so diverse that some historians don't talk about Judaism at the time of Jesus; they talk about "Judaisms" in the plural. The power and pervasiveness of Hellenistic culture would have some impact on Judaism. A few Jews were receptive to aspects of fashionable Greek thought. Many, however, especially in Palestine, wanted to circle the wagons to keep these "pagan" influences from corroding their unique historic Jewish identity.

The Judaism that Jesus knew was divided into theological camps a little like modern religious denominations. Later chapters will show that Jesus constantly came into contact—and conflict—with several of these groups.

The Pharisees

There is an edge of mystery to this sect of Judaism, but it seems that the Pharisees were especially devout Jewish laymen who had at least two related passions. First, they wanted to make it possible for Jews who could not regularly travel to the Temple in Jerusalem to lead fully pious lives. The nexus of Jewish devotion at the time was the great Temple in Jerusalem with its elaborate worship and system of animal sacrifice. But many Jews seldom, if ever, got there. Pharisees sought to expand the devotion and ritual purity associated with the Temple to all Jews, including those who usually prayed only in a local synagogue.

Second, the Pharisees advanced an ideal of scrupulous obedience to the Jewish law, or the Torah. The word "Torah" can mean several things. It can mean the first five books of what Christians call the Old Testament: Genesis, Exodus, Leviticus, Numbers, and Deuteronomy. More specifically, it can mean the laws elaborated in some of those books. (The Pharisees' holy writings included the Torah and the Prophets, as well as later oral traditions.) These rules included not only what we would call moral laws like the Ten Commandments, but they also included or suggested detailed proscriptions about daily routine—everything from how to wash your dishes, to the minutia of keeping the Sabbath day, to questions about whom you could and could not eat with. These rules were aimed to keep Jews "pure" and distinctive, especially in the face of the Hellenistic cultural onslaught. Even though Jesus had much in common with the Pharisees, they would become his bitter foes. Jesus repeatedly aimed verbal blasts at the Pharisees and what their purity laws actually did to people. The Pharisees would come to fear and distrust him as a heretic, and some would play a role in his death.

The Sadducees

The Sadducees were the second Jewish group most often in conversation and conflict with Jesus. The Sadducees were probably smaller in number, and more conservative than the Pharisees, though in a different way. They were members of the priestly cast in Jerusalem, well born and politically influential. They were zealous about the Torah and the maintaining of the traditional practices of the great Temple. In fact, they limited their holy writings to the Torah alone, those first five books of the Old Testament. They denied the doctrine of the resurrection of the dead while the Pharisees affirmed it. More than the Pharisees, the Sadducees, including the high priest and his court, were deeply involved in the push and pull of Jerusalem politics. Jesus would often converse and collide with the Sadducees as well.

The Scribes

This third group, with whom Jesus found conversation and conflict, were not a sect but a professional class. They were men educated in the Torah who could read and write, a rare skill at the time. Because of their literacy and strict piety, people often turned to them for legal and religious counsel and assistance. Some scribes were also Pharisees; some may have been Sadducees.

The Essenes and Zealots

There were other Jewish sects as well, though none of

them clearly played a direct role in Jesus' life. The Essenes, at least one group of whom probably lived in the monastic community at Qumran on the Dead Sea, and who collected the famous Dead Sea Scrolls, withdrew from the world and promoted ascetic practices like celibacy and poverty. Some historians guess that John the Baptist may have either been an Essene or have been influenced by them. The Zealots, as they were later named, are another group about whom little is known. They were not only spiritually zealous for God, but also politically zealous about driving out the Roman occupiers, by violent revolt if need be. One of Jesus' disciples was named Simon the Zealot, to distinguish him from Simon Peter. Some scholars have speculated that Judas Iscariot may have been a Zealot and that he betrayed his master when it became obvious that Jesus was not going to lead an armed revolt against the Romans.

Finally, in addition to these groups that Jesus encountered, there were three other particular aspects of the Judaism of his time that play a part in understanding his life.

The Temple

The spiritual center of Jewish faith at the time of Jesus was the Temple in Jerusalem. Jesus himself visited the Temple and taught in its precincts. The Temple that he knew was the third Jewish Temple to be built on the Temple Mount overlooking the city. It was probably the grandest of the three, and its construction had been started under Herod the Great circa 20 BC. This is the very Herod who would be king of Judea when Jesus was born a decade and a half later and the same Herod who would order the murder of the infants of Bethlehem in an effort to kill the child Jesus. When the adult Jesus visited the Temple and forecast its destruction, it was not yet completed. In fact, it may not have been totally finished when the Romans leveled it in AD 70.

The central act of worship performed in the Temple was the ritual sacrifice of animals, the theological purpose of which was to atone for human sin. The architectural details of the Temple help us understand the Judaism that Jesus knew. Its very layout was emblematic of the ancient Jewish understanding of purity before God. The outermost and most "impure" precinct of the Temple area was called the Court of the Gentiles. Anybody was welcome, even Gentiles or non-Jews. Next came the Court of the Women, where Jewish women might go with their husbands. Deeper toward the Temple itself came the Court of Israel, where Jewish men, but not women, might go. Nearest to the Temple was the Court of the Priests, and inside all these courts was the Temple itself, where only certain priests might go. At the very core of the Temple was a room called the Holy of Holies, containing the symbolic throne of God. The architectural metaphor at work here was one of gradients of purity or holiness before God—Gentiles farthest away and God alone at the center. Though Jesus never spoke about these curious details, his life, death, and resurrection would resist this spiritual geography.

The Torah

An equally important aspect of Judaism, then and now, is Torah, a word that can mean "law" or "teaching," or refer to the first books of the Old Testament. Though the word allows some range of meaning, the core was this: God gave Israel the Torah as a gift. Law is the way for Jews to live obediently before God and to make secure their identity as a unique people among all the people of the earth. For many Jews in Jesus' time, Torah was understood as a way to be pure in the way God is pure. By Jesus' time, there was a strengthening emphasis on the Torah—on reading it, memorizing it, interpreting it, reverencing it, and in keeping it in every last, often punctilious, detail.

The End of the World

The age in which Jesus lived was rife with speculation about the great crisis that many thought was coming soon, perhaps the end of history itself. In times of oppression, Jews, like other peoples, had often visualized a climactic act by which God would rescue the people from their oppressors and usher in a new age. There was a long-standing tradition in Jewish thought about the coming "Kingdom of God," but the years just before and after Jesus saw an explosion of such thinking among Jews, and later among Christians. This kind of thinking and writing is called eschatology, from the Greek *eschatos* and *logoi*, meaning "words about the last." It is a way of thinking that is often jarring to us today, yet such thought was very popular at the time and would influence the way Jesus preached his message.

Each of these—Temple, Torah, and eschatology—are important to understanding Jesus. Near the end of his life, when he taught in the Temple courtyard, Jesus would hint that he himself was the new Temple; that is to say, the place where God and humanity meet. Time and again in his life, Jesus would affirm the importance of Torah, even while pushing beyond its narrow interpretations. And, finally, if any one idea is at the heart of Jesus' message, it is that term often on his lips: "The Kingdom of God." These are words with roots in eschatology, but ones that Jesus interpreted afresh to mean something quite distinct.

How We Know About Jesus

Nearly all of what we know about Jesus comes from the four books at the beginning of the New Testament called gospels, an Old English translation of a Greek word, *euangelion*, which simply means "good news." But even though most of what we know is contained in just four books, we actually know much more about Jesus than we do about most ancient figures of history. There are indeed other ancient documents that offer some additional information, though they add rather little to the picture. Nevertheless, it is important to give them their due.

Ancient Pagan and Jewish Historians

Several ancient pagan historians mention Jesus, all of them in passing. The only historian writing in the first century to offer substantial information about Jesus is the Jewish writer Josephus. In his book *The Antiquities*, he notes that Jesus lived, was a "wise man," a "doer of startling deeds," and "a teacher." He then says that Pilate condemned him to the cross and that many people still follow him.

The New Testament Other Than the Four Gospels.

The second part of the Christian Bible, the New Testament, contains twenty-seven books, the first four of which are Gospels, written specifically about Jesus. The fifth book of the New Testament is a history of the early church during the years just after Jesus that is called The Acts of the Apostles, or "Acts" for short. After that book, the New Testament includes a collection of twenty-one letters called epistles, (from the Greek *epistole*, for "letter.") Most of them were written by Paul, a Greek-speaking Diaspora Jew who had belonged to the Pharisee party, and who became a Christian even though he had never met Jesus in the flesh. Finally, there is the Book of Revelation, a dramatic and poetic example of the then-popular writing about eschatology or "end times." Of all these books, only Paul writes much about the life of Jesus, and that is surprisingly little. He seems to simply assume that his readers know the story. He does, however, confirm the general outline of the story of Jesus' death and resurrection as the Gospels tell it, as well as offering some additional information about the Last Supper.

Christian Writings Not in the New Testament.

The twenty-seven books of the New Testament are not the only ancient Christian writings about Jesus. In fact, there are dozens of other books, most of which call themselves gospels or epistles, as well as fragments of books long lost. Many of these writings have come to light only in the last century. Scholars have poured over them to see if they might offer additional reliable information about Jesus. Though there are sharp differences of opinion among some experts, the consensus is that these other writings about Jesus were written much later than the four Gospels in the New Testament and that they are not generally reliable or independent accounts of what he did and said.

Why Four Gospels?

In the centuries after Jesus, the church realized that it would have to decide which of this flood of gospels and epistles were faithful to the truth about Jesus. They made the decision based on several criteria: Is the book really ancient, meaning can it be traced back to people who knew Jesus firsthand, or at least secondhand? Is the book used in many churches in many places, or is it limited to a few? And, finally, does what the book teaches fit with the basic understanding of Jesus as laid out in most other writings about him, or does it teach things that disagree with the story of Jesus as it has been passed down from his first followers? By the end of the second century, consensus had led to the twenty-seven books that we call the canon (from the Latin *canon,* for "measuring stick") that are included in the New Testament.

The real wonder of the New Testament canon is not that those other epistles and gospels were left out. The real wonder is that the church included four Gospels that tell the story of Jesus in four different ways rather than settle on just one. Early on, some skeptics had criticized Christians for not being able to get their story straight. In fact, there was a move to edit the four Gospels into one book (not something you can do without utterly bowdlerizing them). The idea was to have "one straight story" of Jesus, even if it was a cut-and-paste job. To its credit, the church resisted the effort and insisted that Christians would know Jesus better by reading different versions of his story.

Four Versions of One Story

These four Gospels are the Gospels according to Matthew, Mark, Luke, and John. Gospels are not biographies as we think of that literary genre. Biographies tell the story of the subject's entire life. The Gospels focus on the last few years of Jesus' life. In fact, about a quarter of each Gospel focuses on just the last week of his life. Biographies try to understand how the subject's thinking and actions develop from upbringing, education, and experience. The Gospels are not very interested in Jesus' personal development. Finally, biographies are supposed to be objective, treating the subject's life with some measure of neutrality. The Gospels, on the other hand, were written by writers passionate about Jesus and convinced that he was no mere teacher, but one sent from God. They look back at Jesus' life though the news of the resurrection and unapologetically invite their readers to come to the same faith they have found.

The Gospels of Matthew, Mark, Luke, and John each have their own theological and narrative vantage point, and it's from that particular viewpoint that each tells the story of Jesus in a unique way. The first three Gospels are similar to each other and are called the synoptics (from the Greek *synoptikos*, for "seen together"). John's Gospel is distinctively different. It is helpful to begin with a quick sketch of the unique way each tells the story of Jesus.

Mark: Short and to the Point

The Gospel according to Mark is the shortest and almost surely the first of the four to be written. In its present form it might have been written as early as AD 50. Early church tradition ascribed the book to a young man named Mark, or John Mark, whom we know to have accompanied Paul and perhaps Peter as they told the story of Jesus in their later travels.

The book is written in a fast-paced, almost journalistic style. Mark's favorite word seems to be "immediately." Mark begins his story with Jesus' baptism by John the Baptist. He tells us nothing about Jesus' birth or youth. Jesus' ministry is presented as a life-and-death show-down with the powers of darkness in the world. Jesus' disciples are portrayed in a surprisingly negative light. They never seem to understand his message, they bicker with each other, and scatter at the end.

The original ending of Mark's Gospel was so discomfiting that several later editors actually added more felicitous conclusions. In the blunt way Mark probably originally ended his Gospel, the first witnesses to Jesus' resurrection flee in fear and say nothing about what they saw. Ironically, the only confession of faith at the end of the book is articulated by a Roman soldier standing at the foot of the cross. Mark is a spare, subtle, and sophisticated writer who often uses irony, as well as other literary techniques, to convey his message.

Matthew: History Matters

Even though it was written a decade or more after Mark, Matthew's Gospel was probably placed first in the New Testament because it offers a unique continuity with the Old Testament. More than the other three, Matthew is eager to point out ways in which Jesus is linked to Jewish tradition and is the fulfillment of Jewish hopes for the coming of a Messiah. Old Testament prophets had hinted that God would one day send an "anointed one." "Mashiah" is the Hebrew word for "one who has been anointed," a word later rendered into Greek as *Christos*, or Christ. In contrast to what many assume, "Christ" is not Jesus' second name, but a theological title.

Matthew begins his book with a genealogy tracing Jesus' lineage back through the ancient king of Israel, David, all the way to Abraham, the father of the Hebrew people. Matthew and Luke are the only Gospels that tell us about Jesus' birth. Matthew alone tells the story of the Magi, or Wise Men, visiting the child Jesus.

Matthew's Gospel includes five discourses—longer speeches much like sermons—including the famous Sermon on the Mount. Matthew's telling of the resurrection is much more extensive that Mark's. His Gospel concludes not with Mark's pregnant ambiguity, but with the Risen Christ charging his faithful followers to bring his message to the world and making the stirring promise that he will be with them "to the close of the age."

Luke: Remember the Poor

Luke is the only Gospel that is not a stand-alone book. It's actually the first of a two-volume set, the second being the Book of Acts. The books were separated by later editors who wanted to keep the four Gospels grouped together and to position John's last. Both Luke and Acts are addressed to a reader named Theophilus, meaning "lover of God" in Greek. Luke probably wrote his two-part book at roughly the same time as Matthew, a decade or two after Mark, sometime in the last quarter of the first century.

Though both Luke's books, like the other three Gospels, are anonymous, both have traditionally been attributed to a companion of Paul named Luke who is mentioned several times in Acts. Luke's Greek flows in an especially literary style. Many guess that the writer of this Gospel may have been the only Gentile author of one of our four Gospels. Luke begins and ends his Gospel on resoundingly joyful notes. The climax of Jesus' birth story is the angel's greeting to the terrified shepherds on Christmas night, "Be not afraid, for I bring you good news of great joy." The very last verse of Luke's Gospel tells us that just after the Risen Christ had appeared to them, his disciples "returned to Jerusalem with great joy."

Three other central themes reoccur in Luke. First, he is concerned to show that the message of Jesus is not only addressed to Jews, but to Gentiles as well. Second, Luke is eager to emphasize Jesus' persistent love for the poor and the marginalized of society. Third, Luke, more than the other Gospels, is careful to tell us that Jesus' story included women, that Jesus took women seriously as conversation partners, and that he even included women among his followers. Indeed, Luke tells the story of Jesus' birth from the perspective of Mary, Jesus' mother, and most of what we know about Mary Magdalene, one of Jesus' female followers, comes to us from Luke.

John: A Distinctive Gospel

John's Gospel is markedly different from the other three in both organization and content. Many scholars believe that even though John's Gospel was the last to be written, probably in the last decade of the first century, John based his account on other ancient traditions as well as one or more of the three Gospels that had already been written. More than the others, John's Gospel is obviously "theological," wading deeper into the world of ideas. Jesus is portrayed as human, but John's narrative allows Jesus' divinity to shine through in much more transparent ways.

John tips his hand in his first chapter, in a passage called the Prologue. Instead of offering the reader a birth story with earthy details like shepherds or Magi, he speaks of Jesus coming into the world in beautifully fashioned, even lyrical theology: "And the word became flesh and dwelt among us, full of grace and truth." As mentioned earlier, the "word" (*logos*) in that passage was a venerable Greek philosophical term, though it was also an idea many Jews would have known, because the Torah, or Jewish Law, was often spoken of in such a lofty way. John's Gospel begins to develop ideas that will later become formalized as the doctrines of the Incarnation and Trinity. John also likes to use the "either-or" language of sharp dichotomy; between "light and darkness" and "flesh and spirit," for instance.

In the first three Gospels, we hear about the adult Jesus making only one trip from his native Galilee to Jerusalem. In John, we learn of several. John never has Jesus tell a single parable, the most common form of his teaching in Matthew, Mark, and Luke. Rather, in John's Gospel it is the very actions of Jesus that become enacted parables, or "signs," as John names them. John's Gospel can be divided into two sections, the Book of Signs and the Book of Glory. In the first section, Jesus offers seven of these miraculous signs: changing water to wine at a wedding in Cana, healing a Roman official's son, healing a paralyzed man, feeding the five thousand, walking on water, healing a blind man, and raising Lazarus from the dead. The only one of these signs in the other Gospels is the feeding of the five thousand (where the crowd estimate is four thousand).

This Book of Signs section also includes two extended conversations. The first is a conversation with a devout Pharisee named Nicodemus about being "born again" or, more accurately, "born from above." The second is an even longer conversation with a disreputable Samaritan woman at a well.

One of the literary techniques John often uses is to have Jesus' listeners misunderstand what Jesus says the first time. For instance, after Jesus tells Nicodemus that he must be "born from above," Nicodemus asks a patently foolish question about crawling back into his mother's womb. This offers Jesus the opportunity to speak again and deepen Nicodemus' and the reader's understanding of what he first said.

The second section of John's Gospel, the Book of Glory, focuses on Jesus' impending crucifixion and resurrection. This section includes long discourses in which Jesus speaks to and prays with his disciples, especially on the night before his death. He often talks about "the hour" and his "glory," both of which refer to his coming crucifixion. John wants us to see that it is this approaching act of radical self-giving that reveals the glory of God, and does so in a much more profound way than any conventional demonstration of divine power might. In a sense, Jesus death and resurrection thus becomes John's eighth sign.

How the Gospels Were Written

The best guess as to *why* the Gospels were written is obvious enough. Thirty-some years after Jesus' death, many of the eye-witnesses to his life were beginning to age and die. They had probably been relied upon to pass on the story of Jesus orally. Like most cultures in which few could read, people were adept at extraordinarily accurate memorization. Most scholars believe that some accounts of Jesus had also been written down, perhaps during his lifetime or soon after. These brief written accounts and those verbal memories, both first and secondhand, became the "notes" from which the Gospels were written.

The consensus among most New Testament experts about exactly *how* this happened is called the two-source theory. It's an intriguing puzzle with a deft solution, and even though not every scholar subscribes to it, it's very widely held. In quick outline, the two-source theory goes like this. Matthew and Luke both contain most of what Mark wrote, often word for word. So, the theory is, they probably borrowed right out of that oldest Gospel, making Mark the first source of the two-source theory. But, Matthew and Luke, both much longer than Mark, also contain many virtually identical passages that are *not* in Mark. Where did they get these passages? The logical surmise is that both Matthew and Luke had access to some mysterious, now lost document or set of ancient notes that scholars call "the Q source." (A German scholar first worked this out; the German word for "source" is *quelle*, hence the "Q.") So according to this theory, the second source is long-lost "Q."

Remember, the Gospels were written in a culture that was not concerned about modern copyright issues or what we would call plagiarism. None of the four

Gospel writers even attached their names to their work. Borrowing from other witnesses was simply a way to tell the story truly, and telling the story of Jesus, not authorial credit, was their only concern. So, as the two-source theory has it, Mark wrote first, and Matthew and Luke wrote some years later, borrowing from both Mark and the mysterious Q source. Matthew and Luke also each have some passages, but not as many, that are unique to each of them only. Scholars often talk about these sections as being from the M (for Matthew) source, or the L (for Luke) source. Finally, John's Gospel, so utterly distinct, was written largely independently of the others, even though its author sometimes betrays knowledge of at least one of the other three.

Birth

The story—Luke's telling of it anyway—begins not with Jesus' birth, but with another birth nearly as strange, that of his cousin John. It will be John who some thirty years later will prepare the way for Jesus to do what he is called to do. Luke starts the story with a Jewish priest named Zechariah and his wife, Elizabeth, both advanced in years and childless.

Old Zechariah was struck dumb in the Temple when told by the angel Gabriel that Elizabeth would bear a son whom they were to name John. In a few months, Gabriel returned to make a second annunciation, this more famous one to a young girl named Mary, engaged but not yet formally married to Joseph. Gabriel greeted Mary with words that would become bitterly ironic three decades later, "Hail, O favored one." Gabriel spoke words that angels often speak in the Gospels, "Do not be afraid." Remember that "angel" simply means messenger. No wings, no white robes, indeed no physical description is offered, only the voice. Mary answered with obedience to the utterly unfathomable ways of God, "Behold, I am the handmaid of the Lord."

Several months later, Mary visited her much older pregnant cousin Elizabeth. In the course of the visit, the life in Mary's womb quickened and Luke, whose story this is, records her speaking a beautiful poem, both prophetic and Psalm-like. Its traditional name, the Magnificat is from the Latin of the first word that Mary utters, "magnifies." Her words foreshadow a theme woven through Luke's Gospel: the reversal of power. Mary, young, poor, and a woman, is herself a sign of marginality and powerlessness. In her poem, she sings praise to the God who "has put down the mighty from their thrones, and exalted those of low degree."

When John was born, his father, Zechariah, found his tongue and spoke poetry in the spirit of Mary's more famous Magnificat, saying to his newborn son, "And you, child, will be called the prophet of the Most High; for you will go before the Lord to prepare his ways." "And the child grew . . . ," Luke tells us, and "he was in the wilderness." This is exactly where we will find John three decades later.

The first chapter of this book began with the next story, Luke's version of the birth of Jesus. The details of the tale are worn so familiar that their razor-sharp edges have become blunted: a mother young and poor, of no station, half married; a birth during the night in her husband's ancestral village of Bethlehem sixty miles away from home. Luke offers but two clues to the specific site of the birth. First, he tells us there "was no place for them in the inn," and, second, that Mary laid her newborn son "in a manger," an animal feeding trough. There is no mention of an innkeeper or animals, no stable for that matter. All these familiar and lovely Christmas details are but later surmise.

Angels appeared again, this time to shepherds who, Luke tells us, "were out in the fields." One announced the birth of "a Savior, who is Christ the Lord," and that it had taken place in "the city of David." This angel spoke two titles for the child in one brief announcement, when the child Jesus was named "Lord" and "Savior," two words that would form the core Christian affirmation about who Jesus was for the next two thousand years. The angel also offered a link to the past, saying that this child was born not just anywhere, not in Nazareth where you might expect, but in Bethlehem, the ancestral city of David, that greatest monarch of Israel's golden age.

The fact that the announcement was made to shepherds matters symbolically because shepherds were stationed on one of the lower rungs of Jewish society at the time. The ages have romanticized them, but shepherds were rustics of the most unwashed variety, whose profession probably kept them from keeping the purity laws that made one more respectable. How deeply ironic it is that with so many more suitable members of society doubtless eager for angelic visitation—prominent Sadducee families; devout Pharisees, those resplendent members of the royal court a few miles away in Jerusalem—God should choose shepherds, of all people.

Just where those shepherds were at the time offers us a clue about just when Jesus may have been born. No one knows for sure what time of the year it was. Nowhere does the Bible tell us. Luke only notes that on the night of his birth "shepherds were out in the field," a detail which some scholars believe hints at spring. December 25 was later selected to celebrate Jesus' birth, a date that was thought to be the shortest of the year: the day the darkness began to weaken and the light began to return. As such, it was a powerful echo of the Gospel of John's understanding of Jesus Christ as the Light that "shines in the darkness, and the darkness has not overcome it." In antiquity, December 25 was also the day of the notorious Roman Saturnalia festival, a pagan holiday that, among other things, celebrated the reversal of power, a theme resonant with a poor and vulnerable infant laid in a borrowed manger being Lord and Savior.

Luke ends his story of the birth of Jesus eight days later with the child's presentation at the Temple in Jerusalem for circumcision. There he was recognized and greeted, not by the chief priests but (again ironically) by two codgers who hung around the Temple precincts: a wizened prophet named Simeon and an old woman (a woman!) named Anne. "And the child grew," Luke concludes his infancy story, "and became strong, filed with wisdom; and the favor of God was upon him.

The only other version of Jesus birth is found in Matthew's Gospel, and it offers a distinctively different slant on the story. After Matthew's long genealogy, he too tells of an angelic announcer. His angel did not visit

Elizabeth or Mary, however, but came in a dream to Joseph, to whom Mary was betrothed. Betrothal meant the couple and their families had agreed to marriage and that dowry terms had been settled, but each remained in their own home until the formal marriage. Though they were not yet technically married, custom considered them husband and wife. This angel did not announce pregnancy. Joseph already knew, and had resolved to break the engagement, a step akin to divorce. This angel told Joseph that Mary's pregnancy was not the result of the infidelity he assumed, but that it was "of the Holy Spirit." Matthew says that Joseph had planned a quiet divorce because he was "a just man and unwilling to put her to shame." Odd as it seems, this was probably gracious on his part, as the normative course of action in such circumstances would have been the public humiliation of the pregnant woman. Actually, the law permitted her stoning. Matthew, faithful to his concern for continuity with Hebrew heritage, quotes the Old Testament prophet Isaiah: "All this took place to fulfill what the Lord had spoken by the prophet, 'Behold, a young woman shall conceive and bear a son, and his name shall be called Emmanuel.' " Emmanuel is Hebrew for "God with us."

The familiar center of Matthew's story of Jesus' birth is the visit of the Magi, or Wise Men. They came from "the east." Not very specific geography. The term "Magi" was generally used to denote members of a caste of priestly astrologers and interpreters of dreams from Persia, today's Iran. Whoever they were, they were following a star and arrived not in Bethlehem, but in Jerusalem, just where you would search if you were looking for the newborn king of the Jews. They were received by King Herod, that shrewd and ruthless builder of the Temple. He feigned interest, but as the present king of the Jews, he was more than a little anxious about astrologers come in search of the *next* king. He checked with the experts, who told him that the Messiah, should he come, would be born in Bethlehem. He sent the Magi off to Bethlehem with a sly "Oh, by the way, when you find him, let me know so that I might worship him, too." The Wise Men found the child and his mother "in a house" (not a stable) and fell down before him, offering their famous gifts of frankincense, gold, and myrrh. A dream cautioned them to steer clear of Herod and they avoided Jerusalem on the way home.

The story never tells us how many Magi there were. There might have been two or two dozen. Three gifts are named, but the givers are unnumbered. Whatever their number, these Magi were Gentiles with a capital "G." Such classy and apparently wealthy foreigners were visitors every bit as odd and unlikely as Luke's unwashed shepherds. The narrative point is that these great and wise ones from so far away had come to a peasant child in a nowhere village. From the larger world of the Gentiles, they came to the traditions and promises of little Israel to find what they sought. Their gifts, precious metal and two kinds of incense, were expensive and lavish, offerings fit for royalty. Later notions as to what each might symbolize are but specu-lation.

Matthew ends his version of Jesus' birth with a dark and much less popular tale. Joseph dreamt again, and this time the angel told him to run for his child's life. He took Mary and Jesus to Egypt because Herod, jealous of potential royal rivals, intended murder. This "flight to Egypt" echoes two Old Testament stories, that of the infant Moses' escape from death by floating to safety in a basket on the Nile, and the story of the Jewish nation's epic sojourn and enslavement in Egypt under Pharaoh ,and their return to the Promised Land after the Exodus. Safe though the child Jesus may have been in Egypt, Herod ordered the slaughter of every infant in Bethlehem under the age of two. No despot can ever be careful enough. After Herod's death, Mary and Joseph returned, but not to Bethlehem where Herod's son, Archelaus, at least as dangerous as his father, had now come to the throne. Again at the direction of angelic messengers, they returned to their home village of Nazareth, safely to the north.

Hidden Years

Almost nothing is known about the next thirty years of Jesus' life—almost, but not quite nothing. There are but two clues, the first tiny and enigmatic. Matthew tells us that Jesus' family returned from Egypt to Nazareth so "that what was spoken by the prophets might be true, 'He shall be called a Nazorene.' " That word, "Nazorene" isn't spelled quite right, hinting that it means more than "somebody from Nazareth." It may be a pun on the Hebrew word *neser*, meaning a "shoot," as in the quote from the Old Testament book of Isaiah, "There shall come forth a shoot from the stump of Jesse." Jesse was King David's father, and this passage from Isaiah was long associated with the promise of the Messiah.

Matthew's odd word may also pun another, even more mysterious Hebrew word, *nazir*. *Nazir* referred to a person especially dedicated to God. For example, the famous long-haired Old Testament strongman

Sampson was a *nazir*, or "nazirite." Sampson said of himself, "A razor has never come upon my head; for I have been a nazirite to God from my mother's womb." Either or both ways, Matthew's deft little double pun whispers a bare hint or two about Jesus' hidden years, namely that this child and young man was indeed the promised one, and that during his "hidden years" he grew up devout and radically dedicated to God.

Luke tells us more, but not much more: thirteen verses about Jesus at the age of twelve. At that age, a Jewish boy would assume a man's duties in worship. In two bookend comments to his story of the young boy Jesus, Luke assures us that in these hidden years Jesus grew in strength and wisdom, and in the favor of God and people. Inside those general observations, Luke relates the one specific story we have about Jesus in the years between his infancy and the beginning of his work in his thirties.

Jesus' family went to Jerusalem every year to keep Passover. It's not clear whether Jesus went along every time or if this was his first trip. After their days in the city, perhaps after days of feasting, the family, doubtless in the company of extended family and friends, headed home to Nazareth, a walk of three or more days. After a day on the road, they realized that young Jesus was not among the pilgrims and returned to the city. Following three frantic days, they found him in the Temple among the teachers, "listening to them and asking them questions." Luke tells us that "all who heard him were amazed at his understanding and his answers." Mary, confronting her son as any mother would, said, "Son, why have you treated us so? Behold. your father and I have been looking for you anxiously." His answer was a bold reminder that the Temple was obviously where he should be, and also a play on the word "father." "Did you not know that I must be in my Father's house?"

Where did Jesus study? At home? In the Nazareth synagogue? At some unknown school? Where did he learn scripture so well that he could dazzle the Jerusalem religious professionals at the lean age of twelve? How did he come to be so spiritually focused, so "devoted to God?" How well could he read and write? His first language was Aramaic, and it is clear that he could read Hebrew. He may well have known more than a little Greek, perhaps even some Latin The Gospels answer none of these typically biographical questions, probably because they were simply not considered essential to telling the story of Jesus' work.

We know only that his parents were devout Palestinian Jews. We know that his father and he were craftsmen, perhaps stone masons or woodworkers, though not exactly house carpenters, as houses were not constructed of wood. (The Greek word for their vocation is *tekton*, from which we get "technology.") We know that though Nazareth was a smallish Jewish village, Galilee itself was fairly well populated and contained several cosmopolitan towns that would have had Gentile, Greek-speaking residents.

And, finally, we know that the young man Jesus was spiritually and intellectually focused in a profound way. But from his birth to the day he would walk down to the banks of the Jordan River, some ten rugged miles east of Jerusalem, all else is hidden.

*

Baptism

All four Gospels agree that the first thing Jesus did at the beginning of his ministry was to go to the Jordan River where his cousin John was preaching and baptizing crowds of people. The first three Gospels tell us that John baptized Jesus; the fourth, John, describes their meeting, but never mentions Jesus' baptism. The composite picture the Gospels paint of John the Baptist is clear and consistent.

John was a stunning success as a preacher. Mark says that "all the country of Judea, all Jerusalem" went out to hear John preach; Matthew mentions "many of the Pharisees and Sadducees"; Luke talks about "multitudes who came out to be baptized by him."

John's was a strange character. Mark tells us that he "was clothed in camel hair, and had a leather girdle [loincloth] around his waist." He lived out in the desert and "ate locusts and wild honey." The desert between

Jerusalem and the Jordan River ten miles to the east is extraordinarily rugged and forbidding.

John's main message was simple and delivered with uncompromising bluntness. "Repent!" seemed the point of his every sermon. The meaning of the Greek word found in the Gospels is not quite captured by our English word "repent," however. The Greek implies not so much confessing your sins as it means changing your direction. John was anything but solicitous of his audience, addressing them once as "a brood of vipers."

John's symbol of repentance or "changing direction" was baptism with water. No mention is made of details, whether full emersion under the waters of the Jordan or mere pouring or sprinkling were involved. John did not invent such water ceremonies any more than Jesus did. Water lustration ceremonies had some history in and beyond Judaism. Indeed, they were part of the practice of the Jewish sect at Qumran, which left the famous Dead Sea Scrolls. In John's understanding, baptism was about changing the course of your life and living more faithfully before God and neighbor. For John, baptism might have even been something you did over and over, rather than just once; more scandalously, John seems to have offered his baptism to Jew and Gentile alike.

The second theme in John's preaching was his assurance that he was not himself the awaited Messiah. Rather, John pointed away from himself and toward the Messiah who was coming. John confessed that he was not even fit to stoop down and untie the sandals of this

One who was coming. With more such rhetorical hyperbole, John said that he only baptized with water but that the One who was coming would baptize with fire. All four Gospels tell us that when Jesus approached John at the Jordan, John recognized his preeminence.

The first three Gospels tell us that John then baptized Jesus, and when he did so, God's Spirit descended upon Jesus. Even John's Gospel, which mentions no actual baptism, tells us that the Baptist saw "the Spirit descend as a dove." And finally, in the first three Gospels, a voice was heard, the voice of God declaring that Jesus was God's "beloved Son," with whom God was "well pleased."

The rest of John the Baptist's tale is less familiar. John was slapped in prison by another Herod, the Tetrarch of Galilee and one of the sons of the long-dead Herod the Great. He imprisoned him because John had denounced him for a morally questionable marriage to a woman to whom he was closely related. That woman's name was Herodias, and it was her beguiling dancing daughter who, at the suggestion of her furious mother, asked for the Baptist's head on a platter. But before his death, John questioned his earlier declaration about Jesus and sent several of his own followers to inquire of Jesus, who had now begun his work, whether he, Jesus, was indeed the Messiah or should they "look for another."

The Gospels present Jesus as a man without sin. So why did he need to be baptized? John's baptism was about repentance. What did Jesus have to repent?

Clearly, the meaning of this ancient symbol shifts somewhat when Jesus is baptized. For Jesus and for the Gospels, his baptism became a sign of his "repentance" in the more literal sense of the word: to "change direction." At his baptism, Jesus changed direction, entering into a different relationship with God and turning outward to the world. He was about to embark on a life of preaching and healing, a singular and resolved purpose that would lead him to deadly conflict with the powers of the day. But before he did so, there were temptations to be faced.

Temptation

The first three Gospels say that directly after his baptism, Jesus went into the wilderness for forty days. In all likelihood, it was that harsh wilderness between the Jordan River and Jerusalem. Mark tells the tale in a few lean verses. Mathew and Luke add further details. John never mentions it.

There are several events in the Bible that are forty days or forty years in duration, most famously Noah's flood and Israel's exodus from Egypt. It may be that "forty" is not be taken literally, but was a way to say "a very long time," just as we say a "million" when we want to emphasize the hugeness of a number, even though we don't mean the number literally. The desert and the number forty recall Israel's exodus sojourn, of course. But, more generally, the desert had always been that place of material privation, free of distraction and austere, where people often went to encounter God.

The tempter is named "Satan" by Mark and the

"Devil" by Matthew and Luke. Neither are proper names, and the Bible nowhere offers much of a picture of this illusive evil being. The word "Satan" means "adversary" or "accuser" in the courtroom sense. "Devil" is the English corruption of the Greek diabolos, which means "the one who throws things all over the place."

Matthew and Luke list three specific temptations—to turn desert stones into bread, to leap from the pinnacle of the Temple in Jerusalem to be caught by God's angels on the way down, and to be granted "all the kingdoms of the world"—if only Jesus would fall down before Satan. In each case, Jesus resisted the temptation by quoting a passage of Old Testament scripture in response. Once, Satan responded by quoting scripture back at Jesus, the source of the quip that "even the Devil can quote scripture" to suit his purpose.

The three temptations are both illusive and illustrative. Bread would have obviously satisfied Jesus' hunger, but such a trick might also have enabled him to win the masses with free bread, much in the way Rome at the time kept the restless population of their capital at ease with free bread every day. Jumping from the public and conspicuous pinnacle of the Temple only to be caught by angels would have certainly wowed the crowds. But Jesus was persistently clear throughout his ministry that this was not the kind of faith he sought. The third offer of "all the kingdoms of the world" implies that they were Satan's to hand over. To receive them from Satan would have granted Jesus the earthly, even violent, power to demand faith by dint of edict or threat of sword. Again, this was not the kind of faith he sought.

Jesus rejected the idea of centering his life on material good, rejected the idea of faith gained through spectacular displays, and rejected political power. He now turned to offer faith in a new way.

First Sermon, First Rejection, First Disciples

First Sermon

In the first three Gospels, Jesus began to preach his message right after the temptation experience and just after he had heard that John the Baptist has been arrested. He went home to Galilee, though not at first to Nazareth. Mark and Matthew summarize his first preaching as one bold declaration and one familiar invitation.

Jesus boldly declared that "the kingdom of God is at hand." These are more subtle words than they sound at first hearing. Though the term "kingdom of God" is, as noted above, eschatological language, it doesn't simply mean the end of the world. More generally, the kingdom of God means that realm where God is sovereign; that place, indeed all places, where God is King.

It is that state in which the Eternal One and the values of the Eternal One reign at the center.

When Jesus said, as he often did, that this kingdom of God is "at hand," did he mean at hand as in "coming soon" or did he mean at hand as in "nearby"? Was he talking about the ministry he was about to begin or about a great climactic crisis through which God would come? Was he talking about heaven or about a new way of life in the here and now? Probably all of the above. As often as he proclaimed the Kingdom of God, Jesus always permitted the term to be understood in several ways. He would speak about specific historical events and an approaching crisis in terms of time, but he would also say, "The Kingdom of Heaven is in the midst of you." That is, right now and right here.

Second, Jesus' first preaching offered a bold invitation, one familiar from the preaching of John the Baptist. Like John, Jesus also invited people to "repent." But, remember, as it was with John, the word didn't so much mean "Say you're sorry" as it meant "Change the direction of your life."

First Rejection

After this initial preaching expedition in Galilee, Jesus went home to Nazareth where he preached in his own synagogue. He received a stunning response from this home crowd—they rejected him outright. "Where then did this man get all this?" they asked each other. Luke offers details about the sermon that invited such hostility. He tells us that Jesus attended his Nazareth synagogue on the Sabbath and was asked to read scripture. He read from Isaiah, a passage that says, "The Spirit of God is upon me, because he has anointed me to preach good news to the poor. He has sent me to proclaim release to the captives and recovering of sight to the blind, to set at liberty those who are oppressed, and to proclaim the acceptable year of the Lord." Luke tells us that he closed the book, sat down, and said, "Today this scripture has been fulfilled in your hearing." He meant fulfilled in *himself*. He meant that he would offer a closeness to God never experienced before, a way to God through his own person and life. When the crowd heard this, all hell broke loose. They drove him out of the synagogue, out of town, and mean to throw him over a cliff. Matthew's and Mark's versions of the story slide over these details and simply say "they took offence at him."

First Disciples

Jesus next began to call disciples, a term then used to describe students who would study with either with a rabbi or a pagan teacher. Jesus' disciples were students of a different kind, however. First, typically disciples chose their rabbi, but all four Gospels agree that Jesus chose his disciples. These disciples did not have academic aspirations, but spiritual hunger. They did not long to be great religious scholars; they had simply been captivated by the presence and words of Jesus. There was no classroom, only the road.

Though Jesus clearly had many more than twelve disciples, including a number of women, the Gospels speak of "the Twelve" as being his core followers, a number clearly chosen to echo the twelve tribes of Israel in the Old Testament. These disciples were not all called at once, but singly or in small groups over the first period of Jesus' ministry in Galilee. A few, including Peter, who would become chief among the disciples, were Galilean fishermen. One, Matthew, seems to have been a tax collector, a dishonorable vocation at the time as it implied both dishonesty and complicity with the Roman occupiers. The first three Gospels and the Book of Acts each offer a list of the Twelve, though the names vary slightly. Here is a list compiled from Mark and Matthew, with a note on the slight variations found in Luke and Acts.

Simon (renamed Peter, or Simon Peter)
James
John
Andrew
Philip
Bartholomew
Matthew
Thomas
James, the son of Alphaeus
Thaddaeus
Simon the Cananaean
Judas Iscariot

(In Luke and Acts, Thaddaeus and Simon the Cananaean are replaced by or named Judas, the son of James and Simon the Zealot.)

Later, these Twelve disciples would often be called the Twelve Apostles. A disciple is a person who learns; an apostle is one sent out to teach. This transition from disciple to apostle took place gradually over the years the Twelve were with Jesus, as learners became teachers. Of course, there were disciples other than the Twelve, including many women, such as Mary Magdalene. And there would be apostles other than the Twelve, most famously the apostle Paul.

Ministry

The exact length of Jesus' active ministry has been the subject of much debate over the centuries. The consensus today is that the period of time between that disastrous day in the Nazareth synagogue and the day he entered Jerusalem for the last time was somewhere between one to three years, most likely a little more than two.

Most of these two to three years were spent in Jesus' home district of Galilee, a land of fertile valleys and high hills west of the upper Jordan River. After leaving Nazareth on that fateful day, Jesus seemed to adopt the village of Capernaum, Peter's hometown on the Sea of Galilee (a body of water that figures repeatedly in Jesus' life), as his base.

During Jesus' years of ministry, most of Galilee was ruled at the behest of the Romans by two of Herod the Great's sons; southern Galilee by Herod Antipas and northern Galilee by Philip. A majority of Galilee's residents were probably Aramaic-speaking Jews like Jesus, but there was a significant Gentile population, especially in the larger towns. Jesus left Galilee on several occasions to visit two nearby areas that were veritable "no-go" zones for pious Jews at the time, Samaria to the south of Galilee, and the Decapolis to the east. Samaritans were descendants of the northern tribes of Israel who had intermarried with non-Jews and had developed divergent religious traditions. They were generally disdained by Judean and Galilean Jews. The Decapolis was a string of ten Greek colonies inhabited by Gentile settlers, equally to be avoided.

Although the first three Gospels tell of the adult Jesus traveling to Judea and its capital of Jerusalem only once (during the last week of his life), John's Gospel indicates earlier visits. But, clearly, shortly before a Passover between the years 27 and 33, Jesus, accompanied by his disciples, set out from Galilee to walk south to Judea and Jerusalem. The first place in Judea that we hear of them visiting is the city of Jericho some fifteen arid miles northeast of Jerusalem. Shortly thereafter, on the day we call Palm Sunday, Jesus entered the city from the east riding a borrowed donkey. The next five days, short as they are, were packed with teaching, miracles, intense conversation, and ultimately deadly conflict.

The events that lie inside this two- to three-year period between that sermon in Nazareth and Jesus' entry into Jerusalem on Palm Sunday are impossible to place in definitive chronological order, because their sequence varies significantly in the four Gospels. The

Gospel writers wrote on the basis of memory, perhaps their own and that of others, as well as other documents and earlier collections of "notes."

As is often the case with memory, what happened may be clearly recalled or accurately recorded, but its sequential relation to other events is forgotten as less important. For instance, a person might clearly recall an exceptional Christmas dinner as though it were yesterday, but be unable to remember the year of that particular Christmas. So the Gospel writers organized these events in ways that made the most sense: they grouped the stories of Jesus around common themes, linking them theologically or grouping them geographically. There is, for instance, no way to know for sure whether the story of the healing of the leper happened early in Jesus' ministry, as in Mark's Gospel, or somewhat later, as in Matthew. There is no way to know definitively if Jesus chased the money changers out of the Temple during an early visit to Jerusalem, as John indicates, or in the week before his death, as in Matthew, Mark, and Luke.

The most helpful way to consider the key events of Jesus' years of active ministry is to groups them in the following manner:

1. His message: what Jesus taught in sermons, discourses, and parables

2. His miracles: the acts of healing and other miracles Jesus performed

3. His encounters: the conversations and conflicts Jesus had with people

Even so, these groupings often overlap. For instance, an encounter with someone would often lead Jesus to speak a few words, offer a short homily, or tell a parable. Most of the miracles Jesus performed began with an encounter with a person in need. Then they often became messages or "enacted parables" themselves, not just supernatural deeds.

Jesus spoke dozens of homilies, or discourses, as his short speeches are often called. The first three Gospels record no fewer that thirty-nine parables, and the four Gospels tell us about approximately the same number of miracles. There are at least as many encounters and conversations, some with his disciples, some with adversaries like the Pharisees and Sadducees, and some with curious questioners that Jesus bumped into. Finally, there are a few much longer speeches that might be called sermons.

The next chapters offer an overview of Jesus' message, his miracles, and the conversations he had with those he encountered. A closer focus on a few illustrative examples of each will reveal subtlety and depth that readers often miss, either because the stories are so familiar or because important clues to their meaning have been overlooked.

Message

How Jesus Spoke About Himself

The Gospel of John records a number of short homilies in which Jesus spoke about himself beginning with the words "I am." For instance, "I am the bread of life," "I am the good shepherd," "I am the way, the truth, and the life." Jesus also referred to himself as "the Son"—by implication, son of the Father—several times in John. The term "Son of God" had historically meant simply "one close to God;" indeed it had been used to speak of kings in the Old Testament, and it was even used by Romans to speak of their emperor. In the Gospels, whether on the lips of Jesus or, as is more often the case, on the lips of others, "Son" acquired a loftier and more specific meaning that implies divinity.

But the term that Jesus used more frequently to speak of himself was "Son of Man," a designation shrouded in some mystery. It has roots in the Old

Testament books of Ezekiel and Daniel, as well as some other popular Jewish books not in the Bible that were written in the years just before Jesus. On the lips of Jesus, "Son of Man" was often an indirect way of referring to himself in a manner that emphasized his humanity. The term also had overtones that hinted at Jesus' eventual suffering, the coming crisis in history, and future judgment.

Jesus was addressed by his disciples and most people he met as *rabbi*. *Rabbi* means "my teacher," and it is as a teacher that most people still know Jesus. He taught both his disciples and others in a number of ways. He preferred parables, those pithy stories about daily events that bear spiritual weight. But he also offered a number of short discourses or brief "homilies" as we might call them, and just a few longer "sermons," though the Bible never uses that word.

Homilies and Sermons

On several occasions, Jesus offered instructions to his disciples about what they would soon be facing; for instance, in Matthew 10 and 18, and Luke 9 and 12. He also made brief speeches denouncing the hypocrisy of the Pharisees, as in Matthew 23 and Luke 11. The rhetoric in these passages is razor-sharp. He once compared Pharisees to "whitewashed tombs"; that is, sparking clean on the outside and full of rot and death on the inside. And according to each of the first three Gospels, he offered a brief and ominous apocalyptic homily about the coming crisis, a crisis that might have referred to his death or the end history. Never did he offer his disciples any timetable about the end of the world. Such passages are found in Mark 13, Luke 21, and Matthew 24. Very few words of Jesus are recorded in books of the New Testament other than the four Gospels. One example is in Chapter 20 of the Book of Acts where Paul quotes Jesus as saying, "It is more blessed to give than to receive."

One of the most well-known of Jesus' quotations is actually included only as a footnote in most editions of the Bible. In the eighth Chapter of John, Jesus happened upon a crowd about to stone to death a woman who had been caught in adultery. He said, "Let him who is without sin among you be the first to throw a stone at her." This story is not in the oldest manuscripts of John, and is thought by many scholars to have been included in later editions.

Only twice did Jesus speak words that take up much more than a single page in a Bible: in the Sermon on the Mount in Chapters 5 through 7 of Matthew, and in a long discourse spoken on the last night of his life that is recorded in Chapters 14 through 17 of John.

The first, the Sermon on the Mount, was a public speech. There is, incidentally, a much shorter version of this or a very similar sermon in Chapter 6 of Luke called the Sermon on the Plain.

Unlike the Sermon on the Mount, the long discourse in Chapters 14 through 17 of John was private, addressed to the disciples gathered around him on the last night of his life. It concluded with a long prayer offered on behalf of those followers. It was as part of this long set of final words that Jesus said, "I am the way, the truth, and the life," and that he told his disciples to "love one another as I have loved you."

The Sermon on the Mount

No words that Jesus spoke are better known or have had more lasting impact than those we call the Sermon on the Mount. The name Sermon on the Mount is never used in the Bible. It's derived from the fact that Matthew tells us that Jesus "went up the mountain" to speak. This is a clear parallel with Moses' ascending another mountain to receive the Ten Commandments in the Old Testament. And just as those ancient commandments were quintessentially ethical, Jesus' Sermon on the Mount was ethical to its core.

It is important to understand that Jesus did not mean for his ethics to simply replace the old Law of Moses, the Torah. In the middle of the sermon, he said so clearly, "Think not that I have come to abolish the law." Rather, his sermon was intended to push beyond outward, sometimes hypocritical, conformity or mere rule-keeping and to move his followers toward an inward transformation. The Sermon on the Mount painted a picture of what life lived close to God in the kingdom of God should be like. Its ethics were frankly radical, aimed to do nothing less than turn the common assumptions of the world on their heads. This reversal of the commonly accepted understanding of the world, echoes Jesus' call to "repent," where the word means to turn in the opposite direction.

The sermon opens with the famous list of upside-down blessings called the Beatitudes, a name derived from the Latin translation of the first words of each, "Blessed are . . . " They include "Blessed are the poor in spirit, for theirs is the kingdom of heave," "Blessed are the merciful, for they shall obtain mercy," and "Blessed are the peacemakers, for they shall be called children of God." Luke's account of the Sermon on the Plain offers a similar but slightly different list, including "Blessed are you poor, for yours is the kingdom of God" and "Blessed are you that hunger now, for you shall be filled." These Beatitudes are not precisely commandments, rather they are descriptions of what the blessedness of lives transformed by this message would look like. Like the whole sermon, these words were not a threat—"be like this or else"—but rather a gift that would lead to transformed lives of blessedness, or as the word has sometimes been translated, "happiness." The virtues Jesus blessed were the inverse of the world's de facto values.

Jesus next declared that those who lived in such a way would be the "salt of the earth" and "light of the world." His point was that this new way of living was not just for the sake of the ones who so lived, but for the sake others as well, indeed for sake of the whole world.

The next section of the sermon opened with Jesus' assurance that he had not come to do away with the old Law, but to transform it. The short paragraphs that follow often begin with Jesus saying, "You have heard that it was said . . . " and then noting some traditional commandment, such as against murder or adultery. Jesus then challenged his listeners to go beyond mere outward conformity to these commandments and move toward an inward transformation of the will—an inclination of the heart much deeper than mere obedience to the letter of the law. For instance, Jesus said, "You have heard that it was said, 'An eye for an eye and a tooth for a tooth.' But I say to you, do not resist one who is evil. But if anyone strikes you on the right cheek, turn the other also." In this same section of the sermon, he quoted another law, "You have heard that it was said, 'You shall love your neighbor and hate your enemy.' But I say to you, Love your enemies." It is also here, as well as in the similar sermon found in Luke, that we find the Golden Rule: " . . . whatever you wish that others would do to you, do so to them . . . "

Jesus next instructed the listening crowd about prayer, teaching them the prayer we have come to call the Lord's Prayer. Jesus taught a nearly identical prayer in Luke, but not as part of the Sermon on the Plain. The sermon concluded with several final ethical instructions on matters as down-to-earth as hypocrisy, materialism, temptation, and worry.

The sermon was nothing less than a bold and loving slap across the face. It was meant to startle hearers into asking towering questions about what really makes for a blessed life; that is, a good and happy life of integrity.

Parables

Jesus usually taught by means of short illustrative stories called parables. Jesus did not invent this teaching method; it had a long history in Jewish discourse as well as in other religious traditions. But he was the undisputed master of the medium. There are about thirty-nine parables in the four Gospels. The number is approximate because a few are so brief that they are hardly narratives, but more like simple comparisons or similes. All of them are rooted in the nitty-gritty of life in Palestine. They find their narrative muscle in everyday images of farming, shepherding, weddings, land deals, financial debt, and family troubles.

They were designed to pull even reluctant listeners into the story, to grab them by the collar and lead them to conclusions about life, insights about right and wrong, or an understanding of God that they never expected—and perhaps did not much like. In general, parables are not simple allegories; that is, a person or event in the parable does not necessarily "stand for" a specific historical person or event. Parables are more deft and subtle that that, allowing for various interpretations depending on the concerns and viewpoint of the person hearing it.

The Parable of the Good Samaritan

The most familiar of Jesus' parables are probably the parables of the Good Samaritan and the Prodigal Son. Both are told only in the Gospel of Luke. Jesus told the parable of the Good Samaritan to a "lawyer," that is, an expert in the Jewish Torah, or Law, who had asked Jesus for a precise definition of "the neighbor" Jesus had just told his listeners they were to love. Jesus drew a verbal image of a man traveling from Jerusalem to Jericho, a notoriously dangerous trip. The man is robbed, beaten and left for dead. Three travelers happen by. First a priest, representing the most esteemed religious leadership of the day, then a Levite, a lay associate of that priesthood, and finally a Samaritan. Samaria, as noted earlier, was the region between Galilee and Judea populated by a people called Samaritans, who were judged by the Jewish religious establishment to be ritually impure heretics at least as disreputable as Gentiles. The first two passersby, representative of the spiritual elite of the time, look the other way. Only the unlikely Samaritan shows mercy. He dresses the stranger's wounds and pays an innkeeper enough money to lodge the man for two months. The sharp point is that true religious devotion is revealed more in acts of mercy than in spiritual status or theological orthodoxy.

The Parable of the Prodigal Son

The parable of the Prodigal Son, also told only by Luke, would perhaps better be named "A Father and His Two Sons." We often simplify it by thinking of it as a mere illustration of the forgiveness of God. True enough, but there's much more to be found when you peel back the layers to reveal complex subtleties typical of Jesus' parables.

The background of the telling of the parable is a scene in which some Pharisees and scribes were grumbling about Jesus' habit of welcoming tax collectors and sinners to eat with him, something they didn't think a self-respecting rabbi should do. Pharisees and scribes represented those who lived "right" and, according to the "rules," tax collectors and sinners were those who did not.

The parable tells of a father and his two sons, the younger of whom has the gall to ask this father for his inheritance. He is effectively treating his father as though he were already dead. He takes his premature fortune and heads off to a far (and surely Gentile) land, where he squanders it on loose living. This fast lifestyle and a sudden famine reduce the boy to an entry-level position on a pig farm, a scandalous association with nonkosher pork-on-the hoof that represents a good Jewish boy forsaking his very identity.

He finally resolves to go home and own up to his mistakes, though this decision has a calculated, self-serving edge. He plans what he will say, but when the time comes, his father forgives him before the boy ever manages to get any words out. Running out to meet his son (it was considered unbecoming in that time for a person of dignity to run), this father throws his arms around the boy, kisses him, and tells the servants to bring sandals, robe, and ring, and to kill the fatted calf for a homecoming feast. This extravagance, the very eagerness of the father's grace before the son ever says "Sorry," surely scandalized Jesus' listeners. One sharp point is God's restless, tireless, limitless love for all, even loose-living younger sons, tax collectors, sinners, and Gentiles.

But the story is not over. The Pharisees and the scribes to whom this story was told could hardly miss the allegory as it next circled closer to home. They perhaps saw the tax collectors and sinners mirrored in the prodigal son; they'd be thick if they missed themselves in the older brother. He is self-justifying and proud, whining that he has been "working like a slave" and has "never disobeyed" his father's commandments. He complains that his father never gave him a "young goat" (poorer meat than his brother's "fatted calf") for a party. He lets it slip that he wouldn't have celebrated with his father anyway, just "with my friends." To cap off his righteous rage, he imagines little brother engaged not just in vague loose-living in that far country, but pictures prostitutes, a detail nobody has ever mentioned!

The irony, of course, is that this son who never left home is as lost as his little wandering brother ever was. The final image of the story is this dutiful young man standing outside the feast, the music and the savor of roast veal rising in the night air, his arms, strong from long hours in his father's fields, stubbornly crossed, refusing to attend the homecoming. A story that first seems about the love and mercy of God is suddenly also about spiritual pride and entitlement.

The Great Commandment

No few words of mine would dare summarize the entire message Jesus taught in his brief discourses, longer sermons, and parables. One can, however, trace several themes that arch over all of Jesus' teaching. First, as in the parable of "A Father and His Two Sons," we hear a daring affirmation of the love of God for all human beings, not just certain people or the outwardly righteous. Second, as the Sermon on the Mount teaches, Jesus longed to lead his followers beyond superficial obedience toward a radically deep obedience of the heart.

Also, time and again Jesus spoke to his disciples about the reversal of power, about self-sacrifice—both his and theirs—reminding them that "the first shall be last, and the last shall be first." Increasingly during these years of his active ministry, and as he turned his face toward Jerusalem, Jesus would speak to both the disciples and the crowds gathering around him about the high cost of discipleship. Again and again, he contrasted the world's understanding of greatness and power with the radically different kind of power and greatness that his life, and ultimately his death, embodied.

But when Jesus was asked to sum it all up, he chose one word. In each of the first three Gospels, is slightly different words Jesus was asked the same question: "Which is the greatest commandment in the law?" and each time he offered the same answer. The question was not a technical legal query, rather it was an invitation for Jesus to declare exactly what was at the heart of his teaching. His unequivocal answer was, "Love." The love he spoke about moves in two directions, vertically toward God and horizontally toward others. "You shall love the Lord your God with all your heart, and with all your soul, and with all your mind, and with all your strength." And the second is like it. " You shall love your neighbor as yourself." Neither commandment was original to Jesus. Both are actually in the Old Testament, but no one seems to have ever put them together before. Tradition calls Jesus' answer The Great Commandment.

Miracles

The only non-Christian writer of the first century who tells us very much about Jesus is the Jewish historian Josephus. In his book, *The Antiquities*, he says that Jesus was a "wise man," "a teacher," and a "doer of startling deeds." All these centuries later, most people would echo Josephus' summary of what Jesus did. Jesus taught, and he also performed startling deeds—miracles, some thirty-nine of which are recorded in the four Gospels. But before considering Jesus' miracles specifically, the concept of "miracle" requires some examination.

Miracles Then and Now

The ancient world in which Jesus lived had a dramatically different way of looking at miracles than we do today. Our world tends to see miracles through the lens of what's called the closed-system universe. This is a cause-and-effect worldview that was developed about

250 years ago during the Enlightenment. It portrays the universe as a closed system in which one natural "effect" happens only because of some other natural "cause." If there was a God involved in the original creation, that God has now pulled out of the equation to let the world operate as a system closed to "outside" divine influence. This universe of cause-and-effect relationships could eventually be understood, Enlightenment thinkers hoped, and then emptied of mystery if only we worked at it long and hard enough. If miracles were allowed into this picture at all (which they generally were not) they were understood as violations of the cause-and-effect rule in which God (or some unknown force) broke into the closed system to create an effect that had no cause.

This description of how the universe works, so familiar to us, is simply not how the ancient world looked at things. Miracles were more routinely accepted and were not understood as inexplicable exceptions to the rule but, among Jews and early followers of Jesus at least, as signs of God's purpose in the world and in the lives of individuals. Most of the people who saw Jesus perform miracles were open to the idea that such wonders were part of a mysterious world. The question they were more likely to ask was not "How did he do that?" but "What does it mean?" And, just as interesting, in the last half-century modern science has raised probing questions about the simplistic formulas of the Enlightenment's closed-system universe. As scientific exploration, from biology to physics, has pushed deeper and higher, it has glimpsed a universe more inexplicably mysterious than earlier science had assumed.

Jesus' Miracles

The miracles of Jesus can be divided into several types. First, Jesus performed what witnesses understood to be "exorcisms." Most ancient people considered many problems that we categorize as disease in terms of demonic possession. When Jesus healed a "possessed" person, it was seen as the power of a compassionate God defeating evil powers that were destroying a human life. Many of the cases of demonic possession noted in the Gospels resemble what we now think of as mental illness; in another case we can recognize epilepsy.

Second, Jesus healed people with physical illnesses or deformities. This category includes people paralyzed or otherwise unable to walk, people with leprosy, and several who were blind. Third, there are also three incidents in which Jesus restored to life a person who was dead, or at least thought to be dead: the raisings of the daughter of Jairus, the son of the widow of Nain, and of Lazarus, brother of his followers Mary and Martha. Note that these are not resurrections in the same sense as the Gospels tell of Jesus' resurrection. They are more properly thought of as resuscitations. Lazarus, for instance, though he was brought to life, would die again. Nevertheless, these miracles were signs pointing toward that future resurrection.

Finally, there are a number of miracles, often grouped together under the title "nature miracles," that do not involve the healing or restoration of a person. These include Jesus walking on water, his quieting of the storm, the feeding of the multitude, and the miracle at the wedding at Cana in which Jesus changed water to wine.

Jesus' miracles were not performed in order to manipulate people into believing in him. In fact, the Gospels all agree that his miracles actually had the effect of solidifying resistance to his work. Time and again after a miracle, Jesus told the person he had healed and those who had witnessed the event to tell no one about it. He seemed to want to avoid both popular attention and having people believe in him only as a miracle worker.

Jesus' miracles were signs of the new relationship with God that he was presenting. They were also enactments of a divine compassion that simply could not pass by human suffering without reaching out (often literally) in response. Jesus' miracles, especially his healing miracles, were "living parables" of how a God of love and power could touch a trouble-plagued world and its suffering people. Often, Jesus' miracles were actually dramatized sermons revealing truth in a way more vivid than mere words ever could.

Wine at the Wedding

In the second chapter of John's Gospel, we hear the story of a nature miracle that no other Gospel records. On the surface, the story seems simple enough, but like many miracle stories, the miracle at Cana is deeper than it first appears, layered with meaning and subtly

73

emblematic. Jesus had just called his disciples and they'd been invited to a wedding in a Galilean village named Cana. Halfway through the wedding, the hosts ran out of wine. At first Jesus seemed loath to get involved, but changed his mind and had the household's head servant fill six thirty-gallon jars with water. When the head servant tasted the water, it had turned to wine, fine wine at that, upward of 180 gallons of it, the equivalent of no fewer than seven or eight hundred modern bottles.

On the surface, it seems a straightforward miracle story showing the power of Jesus over the elements. But, as noted earlier, everything is often more than it seems in miracle stories. Water is not just water, and wine is not just wine. In this story, water stands for the "old life." Specifically, the water that Jesus changed into wine was there for the traditional Jewish rites of purification and is thus a symbol for religious legalism. Wine, on the other hand, is a symbol of for the spirit, a metaphor for the potential fullness and goodness of life. So when water became wine, the miracle was not just a conjurer's trick, but a sign telling us that with Jesus at the feast of life, the flatness of the old existence could become new life—rich, full and spirited. Indeed, the copious amount of wine is a symbol of the sheer abundance of God's blessing. Later in the Gospel of John, Jesus will say this plainly, "I have come that they may have life, and have it more abundantly."

Beyond the Pale

The seventh Chapter of Mark's Gospel tells two

provocative healing stories back-to-back. They follow a brief discourse in which Jesus argued that what a person eats (by which he meant food, not on the ritually pure Pharisee diet) cannot defile a person. Rather, what defiles a person is what a person does, his actions in life. The two miracles that follow, the exorcism of a little girl and the healing of grown man with a speech impediment, are not just wonders, but enactments of what Jesus had just said about the whole matter of ritual purity, including the preoccupation the Pharisees and others had with food and its preparation.

These are not especially familiar healing stories, probably because they make us uncomfortable. We are uneasy with miracles in general, of course, but even more uneasy with the first of these because Jesus seemed to decline someone's plea for help and then to change his mind about the matter. Our traditional image of Jesus simply does not imagine him making a distinction on the basis of ethnicity or ever altering his view on anything.

The story begins with Jesus entering the area around Tyre and Sidon, a Gentile region west of Galilee along the Mediterranean coast. A Gentile woman fell at his feet and asked him to heal her little daughter who was "possessed by an unclean spirit." Jesus first said no to the woman, a no that sounded insulting. Jesus told her that the "children" must be fed first, the children being the people of Israel, the Jewish corner of the world. It would be wrong to take bread from the mouths of these first children to feed the dogs, he said. That last word stings, of course. It's actually a diminutive and could be translated as "little dogs" or "puppies," but that only softens the blow only a bit. The point is that Jesus' first priority was the Jewish people and this woman was asking him to shift focus to another world, the world of the Gentiles. But even with these caveats, Jesus' answer surely accents the human side of his nature.

Of course, no was not Jesus' final answer. This was one persistent lady! She had pushed her way into the house, probably past a defensive line of disciples, and now she came back at Jesus with a clever retort. She reminded him, rather caustically it would seem, that even "puppies" get to eat crumbs that fall from the table. At this point Jesus changed his mind, bent to her need, bowed to her importunity, and healed her little daughter.

These two edges—miracles in general and a Jesus who changes his mind—make the story hard to hear in our world. But back then it was a hard story to swallow for a different reason. Jesus had gone to where no self-respecting rabbi ought to go. Jesus was male and a Jew and this story presents him in serious conversation with a person who is female, a foreigner, and a heathen. And if that scandal were not blatant enough, Jesus next had the gall to turn around and head toward yet another Gentile region in exactly the opposite direction, an area called the Decapolis.

The Decapolis was a string of ten pagan Greek colonies that had grown up right in the middle of the Jewish heartland. There Jesus encountered a man, doubtless another Gentile, with a hearing and speech impediment that he healed. Everything in Jesus' religious world militated against both of these contacts. The whole episode had an outrageous edge: a rabbi, a man who was supposed to be a moral example to his disciples, crossed the ancient lines of gender, race, and religion. In these two miracles Jesus not only dramatized the compassion of a God who could not walk past suffering, but a God whose compassion extended further than anyone imagined.

Touching Untouchable

The first three Gospels tell the story of the healing of a man described as a leper. This leper man rather brazenly approached Jesus in spite of the fact that lepers were supposed to keep their distance from the healthy. He prostrated himself before Jesus and told him that he could heal him if he chose to. Jesus stretched out his hand, touched the leper, and healed him. The disease mentioned might refer to a variety of skin ailments, anything from psoriasis to Hanson's disease. Whatever the clinical reality, because the disease was understood to be an emphatic mark of ritual uncleanliness, the Jewish purity laws of the time placed lepers in an internal exile.

But when Jesus touched, *touched*, this leper, he not only healed him, but in the act of touching made himself vulnerable to contagion and rendered himself ritually impure. The irony, of course, is that it was not Jesus who was made unclean by the contact, but the leper who was made clean. Jesus crossed a boundary only to bring the outcast home to physical health and reintegration into society. Again, the miracle was not just a matter of physical healing; it was a dramatized enactment of spiritual reality, namely Jesus' readiness to extend the love and compassion of God beyond established boundaries.

More Than Meets the Eye

Similarly, many of Jesus' miracles are also dramatizations of his message. For instance, the feeding of the multitudes with no more than a little boy's basket of bread and dried fish was not just a miracle, it was also an echo of the story of Moses' feeding the people of Israel with manna during the exodus through the desert, and a general sign that with God there is always enough to go around. To have an better understanding of Jesus walking on water or calming the storm on the Sea of Galilee, you must first know that deep water was a symbol for chaos. For Jesus to calm the storm was not just a trick, but a demonstration of God's ultimate power over the forces of chaotic disorder. The several stories of Jesus healing the blind cannot be understood apart from the fact that physical blindness was a metaphor for being unable to see spiritual truth. To be healed of blindness was also to see the truth that had been hidden.

Encounters

Jesus seems to have traveled almost constantly during his two or three years of active ministry, visiting cities and villages in and beyond Galilee. He and his disciples were on the road most of the time, constantly meeting people, both in groups and individually.

Jesus' reputation grew quickly. We frequently hear of crowds coming out from villages to meet him. At some points, large crowds were actually traveling with him. People were constantly pressing toward him: the ill, those with spiritual questions, the troubled in mind or spirit. Mothers pushed their little children at him for a blessing. A sick woman desperately reached though a jockeying crowd to touch his robe. A diminutive tax collector named Zaccheus climbed a tree in Jericho to get a better look when Jesus passed by.

Often the disciples are described as being protective of Jesus, though he evidenced a welcoming demeanor.

Several times, however, he retreated from the constant clamor of insistent crowds. He was often invited to dine, and was roundly criticized by some Pharisees and scribes for accepting invitations from hosts they considered disreputable. Time and again, he displayed an outrageous hospitality to the most marginalized people. Sometimes he spoke outdoors, sometimes in a local synagogue, sometimes in private homes. Certainly, Jesus' ministry attracted extraordinary attention.

It is impossible to precisely map these journeys. It may be that Jesus was based in Peter's hometown of Capernaum on the Sea of Galilee and traveled from there, often into nearby northern Galilee, less often to southern Galilee where his own hometown of Nazareth was located, occasionally into nearby Gentile areas, and finally, near the end of his life, south through eastern Samaria into Judea. There he stopped in Jericho and then went to Jerusalem to meet the crisis that awaited him there.

One exceptional aspect of the record the Gospels offer of these travels is the sharp and rich details they contain about the encounters Jesus had with people along the way. In fact, they often include something rather unusual for writing in the ancient world—actual dialogue. All four Gospels are peppered with such meetings and the conversations that shape them. In John's Gospel these encounters are fewer and longer. In the first three Gospels they are more numerous and often lead Jesus to offer a brief homily or to tell a parable.

The meetings were of several kinds. First, there were the conversations that Jesus had with his disciples, either all of them together or several at a time. These were often private conversations in which Jesus spoke words meant for the ears of his followers alone.

Second, there were the many encounters with curious, questioning, or troubled individuals. Many of these encounters led to Jesus performing healings or concluded with a parable or a brief teaching. For instance, the Great Commandment of love for God and neighbor was spoken in response to a question put to Jesus from an unnamed lawyer he met one day.

Third, there were some meetings with larger groups of people who came to hear or see him. The Sermon on the Mount was preached to such a large group.

Fourth and finally, there were many encounters with Pharisees, scribes, or, as was often the case, Pharisees and scribes together.

Sometimes these were encounters with individuals, but more often they were with groups of people. During the last week of his life, when he was in Jerusalem, Jesus also met members of the Sadducee sect of Judaism, although the Sadducees are rarely mentioned before Jesus entered the city. Most, but not all, of the encounters Jesus had with scribes and Pharisees were marked by sharp conflict. A closer look at several examples of these different kinds of encounters will help us better understand what Jesus did and who Jesus was.

Doing the Dishes

Mark's Gospel tells the story of what appears at first glance to be an inscrutable confrontation between

Jesus and a group of Pharisees and scribes over, of all things, washing your hands and doing the dishes.

The tale begins when some scribes and Pharisees criticized Jesus' disciples for not ritually washing their hands and dishes. This had nothing to do with hygiene, as the amount of water used in these ceremonies was purely symbolic. The Pharisees called this "a tradition of the elders," meaning that it was not a part of the Torah or Jewish Law itself, but a practice that had gown up to prevent a person from accidentally doing something that might violate Torah laws.

Jesus answered the charges first by quoting a passage from the Old Testament prophet Isaiah about people who obey God with their lips, but not their hearts. Jesus was implying that the Pharisees kept the letter of the law but forgot about what really mattered. He then offered a real-life illustration (real-life two thousand years ago, though perhaps a little remote today) of a son who hatched a financial scheme to defraud his parents on a technicality of religious law. Such a son would be keeping to the letter of some minor law, even though he'd clearly be violating one of the Ten Commandments, "Honor your father and your mother." "What kind of morality is that?" Jesus asked. Having quoted Isaiah and offered a practical illustration, Jesus summed up for the listening crowd. "It's not what goes into you," he implied, "rather it's what comes out of your life that matters." This was a theological arrow aimed right at the Pharisees.

Although this whole matter of washing dishes may seem picky to us, the incident is a micro example of a macro confrontation. It contrasts an earnest but outward religiosity, a reality still with us today, with a faith characterized by real inner transformation. The question behind this odd encounter may still be the religious bottom line: is faith something you wear dutifully on the outside, or it is it a force that changes who you are on the inside?

The Eye of the Needle

The first three Gospels all tell the story of one of the few people to encounter Jesus who said no to him, and it was because of money. A rich man knelt at Jesus' feet, addressed him rather flatteringly, and asked, "What must I do to inherit eternal life?" Jesus answered by bringing several of the Ten Commandments to the man's attention. He responded that from his youth he had kept these laws. Then Jesus looked at him (Mark adds "and he loved him") and told the man to liquidate his holdings, give the proceeds to the poor, and follow him. The man was shocked by the answer and left sadly. But before he went, Jesus noted how hard it is for those who have lots of money to enter the Kingdom of God, that realm where God (not your balance sheet) is on the throne. It would be easier, he added, "for a camel to go through the eye of a needle." "Well, that's impossible!" the listening crowd complained, "Who can be saved?" Jesus answered, "What is impossible for mortals is possible for God."

Several possibilities have been suggested to interpret Jesus' unusual image of the camel and the eye of the needle. Some have guessed that there may have been a small gate into Jerusalem named metaphorically "the Eye of the Needle." Perhaps a camel could pass though it, but only on its knees and relieved of the material burden on its back. A possibility, but there is no hard evidence of any such gate. Others have suggested that the Aramaic word that ends up "camel" in Greek and English actually referred to a kind of coarse thread. Again speculation, though more likely than the gate. Possible as such surmises might be, the clear fact is that Jesus, like most rabbis of the day, was very fond of outrageous rhetorical hyperbole to drive home his point. Time and again, Jesus used the exaggeration to make his message emphatic.

In this encounter, Jesus saw deep into this man and knew what made him tick. Jesus saw that for this particular man wealth had become a stumbling block to integrity. Money was his personal spiritual impediment. The man obviously knew something was missing; he would hardly have thrown himself at Jesus' feet otherwise. Jesus recognized that in the midst of outward abundance, the man lived in an ironic inner poverty that only a radical reordering of his priorities would alleviate.

Peter's Confession at Caesarea Philippi

Matthew, Mark, and Luke each tell the story of the day Jesus asked Peter bluntly who he, Jesus, was. Jesus and his disciples were near the city of Caesarea Philippi. His fame had been spreading, and he asked his disciples who people were saying he was. They answered that popular speculation had it that he was John the Baptist or one of the Old Testament prophets come back from the dead. Unsatisfied, Jesus turned the question at right angles. "But who do *you* say that I am?" Simon Peter answered with the first clear statement that Jesus was the Messiah. The Anointed One. The Christ whom prophets had long promised and Israel had long awaited. Jesus then told them not to say anything about this. Matthew's Gospel adds that Jesus then made a pun on the name Peter, which sounds like the Greek word for rock, by telling Peter (*Petros*) that he was the rock (*petra*) on which the church would be built. This incident is a turning point in the story of Jesus because a declaration was made (from someone other than a writer of a Gospel) that Jesus was not just another rabbi, not just somebody revived for a second appearance, but the One for whom the ages had waited.

A Mother Ambitious for Her Sons

The encounter with Peter and the disciples noted above is one of rather few that shows them in favorable light. More often, when Jesus spoke to his immediate followers it was to tell them two things they didn't want to hear and seemed brilliant at misunderstanding. First, with increasing frequency, he told them that he must go to Jerusalem and there suffer and die. Once when he said this, Peter simply refused to face such a horror. Jesus rebuked him saying, "Get behind me, Satan," meaning do not tempt me to run away from what must be.

Second, Jesus made it clear that to follow him would require that they, indeed all followers, come to a new understanding of power and be prepared to make sacrifices themselves. These frequent speeches drew on various metaphors to drive this uncomfortable truth home. For example, Jesus compared those who would enter the Kingdom to "little children," an unsentimental image in a world in which children were marginal and powerless. He used the jolting imagery of reversal, saying repeatedly that "the first shall be last and the last shall be first." He said that those who "lose their life will find it." Most discomfortingly, he said, again using hyperbole and metaphor, "Take up your cross and follow me."

One very human encounter that concluded with such words is related in Matthew's Gospel. The mother of two of Jesus' disciples, "the sons of Zebedee," came to him and pleaded with him to give her boys good leadership positions in the coming Kingdom. Her notion of Jesus' Kingdom and what such positions in it might mean was so befuddled that we might smile but for the pathos. Jesus told her that she did not know what she was asking. To the "sons of Zebedee" he said, "Are you able to drink the cup that I am about to drink?" It's not clear if they knew what "cup" he meant, but they bravely answered, "Yes." You can almost hear Jesus sigh as he explained yet again what this was all about. "You know that the rulers of the Gentiles lord it over them, and their great ones exercise authority over them. It shall not be so among you; but whoever would be first among you must be your slave." In the last days of his life, Jesus would live out such radical sacrifice in the starkest drama imaginable.

Crisis

In the spring of a year sometime between 30 and 33, probably during what we would now call March or April, Jesus left Galilee and went to Jerusalem. For some months, he had been warning his disciples that the time would soon come for them to go to that great city. Indeed, he had sometimes been ominously clear about what would happen to him once he was there.

The disciples seem to have consistently misunderstood him, or simply refused to believe what he said. The first three Gospels mention no other journeys to the city and leave the impression that this was Jesus' first as an adult; John's Gospel offers it as the third or fourth. In either case, this journey was timed so that Jesus and his disciples would be in Jerusalem for Passover, along with thousands of other Jews who customarily went there for that greatest of holy days, swelling the population many times over.

In Jesus' time, Passover had come to be coincidental with another less important Jewish festival called the Feast of Unleavened Bread. The next five days would see not just the end of Jesus' life, but also the events that defined his ministry and his very identity.

Unlike his years of ministry, the sequence of events during the critical last week are much easier to trace. The first three Gospels chronicle this period, which culminates in what has come to be called the passion (from the Latin word for suffering, *passio*). John's account of the passion adds critical details and omits others.

Transfiguration

But before we come to that last week, we must note one especially enigmatic event that took place during Jesus' years of ministry but was not quite classifiable as message, miracle, or encounter.

Sometime in those two-plus years of active ministry, probably toward the end and somewhere in Galilee, Jesus took three of his disciples, Peter, James, and John, up an unnamed mountain. There Jesus' appearance was somehow altered; "transfigured" is the common English translation of the Greek *metamorphoun*, from which we also derive "metamorphosis." His face shone and his garments appeared unnaturally white. The three disciples saw him talking to two figures from the Old Testament, Moses and Elijah. Peter was so struck that he told Jesus they should stay there and build booths, little places of worship, one for each of them.

But Jesus insisted they leave. Suddenly, a voice from a cloud proclaimed, "This is my beloved son [Luke has 'my chosen'], listen to him." Then, just as suddenly, Jesus was alone again. The three disciples descended the mountain with him, saying nothing about what they had seen.

The physical phenomenon of the transfiguration is not a one we can even begin to comprehend. But we can begin to understand its spiritual significance. First, this event looks to the past. The figures of Moses and Elijah represent heritage and continuity with Jewish history. Moses stands for Torah, or Law; Elijah stands for the prophets. Indeed, Elijah was often associated with the restoration of the fortunes of the nation that so many Jews were longing for. The mountaintop setting and Jesus shinning face also recall Moses' ascent of Mount Sinai to receive the Ten Commandments.

Second, the transfiguration looks to the future, specifically toward the resurrection, where similar physical descriptions will detail an equally and fundamentally indescribable event. Finally, Peter's eagerness to remain on the mountain, lost in a mystical moment, and the fact that Jesus had to lead his followers back down the mountain demonstrate Jesus' insistence that his work, in order to reach its highest conclusion, must include the passion, his approaching passage through suffering and death.

Put another way, if you did not know the whole story of Jesus, the transfiguration might seem a fit place to bring it all to a modestly happy ending—without death, without resurrection.

Entrance

About five days before the festival of Passover, Jesus entered Jerusalem in what appears to be a deliberate and ironic parody of general expectations as to how the real Messiah might do such a thing. He entered the city from the east, riding down the side of the Mount of Olives from its villages of Bethany and Bethphage, through the deep Kidron Valley, and finally up into the city through a gate quite near the Temple. But he did not ride a great stallion. Feet dragging in the dust, he straddled a more humble beast—a colt or a donkey. Behind him marched no army, just a handful of rustic disciples: illiterate Galilean fisherman, an errant tax collector, and several women. He bore no weapon but his piercing word. He rode toward no throne, only toward a cross. And his crown would be fashioned not of gold, but of plaited thorns.

The day we call Palm Sunday cannot be understood without knowing both the larger and the more immediate contexts. The larger context included the then popular messianic hopes that God would send a leader, powerful in the earthly sense, who would liberate the nation from the Roman yoke—by the sword if need be. Such an image is in stark contrast with the image of Jesus' modest entrance into in the city.

The immediate context included a city packed with Passover pilgrims. Religious fervor among these masses of visitors mixed a volatile brew that naturally made local authorities anxious about keeping order. Indeed, the crowds did meet him, and enthusiastically. The exact words they shouted in greeting vary from one

Gospel to another, but they include naming him "King," "Son of David," and calling out "Hosanna!" meaning "Save us!" All were politically provocative words. Some Gospels note that the crowd cut "leafy branches" or "palms" and, along with their clothes, laid them in Jesus' path as you would before a king entering the city. The entrance set the stage for the events to come by making at least two things clear: Jesus was dangerously popular with the people, some of whom clearly regarded him as a king in some sense, and, second, the nature of Jesus' "kingship" was quite unlike anything anyone expected.

The Next Five Days

According to the first three Gospels, the first thing Jesus did upon entering the city was to go directly to the Temple, that most holy of holy sites, that very intersection of the human and the divine in the contemporary Jewish spiritual landscape. Matthew, Mark, and Luke tell us that outside the Temple he confronted moneychangers and sellers of sacrificial pigeons, overturning their tables and chasing them away. (A similar incident is related in John's Gospel, but it is set earlier in Jesus' ministry.) These sellers of pigeons provided small sacrificial animals for a price, creatures worshippers could then offer as atonement for their sins. The moneychangers traded Roman and Greek coins, unacceptable because of the pagan images they bore, for appropriate Jewish ones that could be used by worshippers to make monetary offerings to the Temple treasury. It's not clear whether these transactions were exploitative and corrupt, or if Jesus was simply denouncing a religious devotion devolved into mere business. What is clear is that the pitch for the days to come had been set, and it was sharply confrontational.

The Temperature Rises

The next five days included all those elements of the first years of Jesus' ministry—preaching, healing, and encounters—but now every event heightened conflict and raised tension. Jesus predicted and lamented the destruction of the city; he cursed a hapless and fruitless fig tree that symbolized barren religiosity. He told parables that were thinly veiled critiques of the religious establishment. He debated with the Temple's chief priests and elders about true authority. The Pharisees tried to entrap him with a question about paying taxes with Roman coins bearing pagan images. His famous answer to their question was, "Give therefore to the emperor the things that are the emperor's, and to God the things that are God's."

On another occasion, others tried to corner him with that question about which is the greatest of all the commandments in the Law, a question he answered by articulating the Great Commandment to love God and neighbor. He debated with the Sadducees about the resurrection, a doctrine in which they did not believe. In a long homily bound together by the repeated refrain, "Woe to you!" he lambasted the Pharisees for hypocrisy. He preached stark homilies, apocalyptic and ominous in tone, about the crisis to come. He told several parables about the need for watchfulness and the importance of being prepared.

During these several days, Jesus' pattern was to return each night to the village of Bethany on the Mount of Olives east of the city where he was staying with friends. Needless to say, the combination of Jesus' frank and jolting preaching, his uncompromising words to and about the religious powers in the city, his significant popularity, the political tensions between Romans and Jews, the widespread messianic expectations, all set within a city teeming with passionate religious pilgrims, proved to be not just dangerous, but deadly.

Passion

Conspiracy

Jesus had often spoken of the inevitability and necessity of his death. His enemies actually began to plan for it a day or two, perhaps longer, before the Passover holiday on which it would occur. The plot seems to have started not among the Pharisees with whom relations had often been tense, but among the "chief priests," the "elders of the people," and the "scribes." This overlapping group represented the local Jerusalem elite, the religious and political power structure in the city, subject of course to Roman authority vested in the governor, Pontius Pilate. These elders and chief priests conferred together about how to arrange to have Jesus arrested and killed, but even as they did so, they were deeply anxious about how such a move might be viewed by the common people, especially during the Passover when the city was full of pilgrims. The next important turn of the plot was the connection with Judas Iscariot, that disciple of Jesus who would betray his master. But before Judas' betrayal, several of the Gospels tell the story of an incident in utter contrast to that impending betrayal.

On what was probably Wednesday evening, in the village of Bethany outside Jerusalem, Jesus was in the home of one "Simon the leper." While at dinner, an unnamed woman entered the house with a jar of expensive perfume and anointed Jesus' head with it. The disciples indignantly bemoaned the cost, noting that it could have been sold for a fortune and the money given to the poor. Jesus however, defended her and interpreted the act as a harbinger of his impending death. Just as the bodies of the dead were anointed for burial, she had anointed him. Then, for reasons never explained, Judas went to the chief priests and arranged to help them find and identify Jesus so that they might arrest him.

Passover/Last Supper

The story advances to the next day, the Day of Unleavened Bread. According to the first three Gospels, this is the day when, in the evening Passover would begin; Thursday by our reckoning. (According to Jewish custom, days begin not during the night or in the morning, but at sundown.) Jesus instructed several of his disciples to go into Jerusalem and arrange for the keeping the traditional Passover meal in an "upper room."

Matthew, Mark, and Luke narrate the events of that night and the next day from much the same angle of vision; John's Gospel tells the story from a typically distinct point of view. According to the first three, the Passover meal began with Jesus' lament to his gathered disciples that one of them would betray him. The story moves immediately to Jesus' dramatic reinterpretation of the Passover meal at which they were seated, probably not on upright chairs, but reclining as was the custom. This meal had traditionally recalled God's providential delivery of the people of Israel from slavery, and their salvation from death in Egypt through the Exodus. But Jesus took the Passover bread, saying "This is my body." And then the Passover cup of wine, saying "This is my blood." With these words he proclaimed that his life and his death, indeed his message and very being, would deliver the people and save them in a new way.

In the Gospel of John, however, no mention is made of such words, words what have come to define the Christian sacrament of Communion, also called the Eucharist (meaning "thanksgiving") or Lord's Supper. Instead, John tells the story of how Jesus rose during the meal and washed the feet of his disciples. Washing the feet of guests was common hospitality in that world of sandals and dusty roads, but it was a task routinely assigned to a lowly household servant or slave. Jesus' act turned the world's common understanding of service and power on its head. Peter initially resisted letting Jesus wash his feet, but he relented when Jesus interpreted the act to him. All the Gospels tell us that at that Passover table Jesus specifically predicted Judas' betrayal.

Jesus then prophesied that his other disciples would soon scatter and that Peter ("the Rock") would deny him three times before the cock crowed, (before dawn of the next day). This second prediction of disloyalty among his followers happened either while they were still in the upper room, on their way to, or as they arrived at the Garden of Gethsemane on the Mount of Olives just east of the city across the Kidron Valley. It was to this garden, perhaps a quiet olive grove that Jesus went to pray after the Passover dinner, just as he seems to have done before. His disciples followed him, and there he was betrayed and arrested.

Arrest

The early part of the scene in the garden includes a portrayal of Jesus engaged in agonized prayer on the eve of his death. Two Gospels record him praying, "My soul is very sorrowful, even to death." He requested of God that "this cup" (death) be removed from him. The first three Gospels also tell us that at this point of supreme crisis his waiting disciples did nothing but fall asleep.

Jesus woke them just in time for the arrival of Judas leading "a crowd" (as the first three Gospels name those who come to arrest him) of "the chief priests and the elders." Mark also includes "the scribes" on the list, and Luke adds "the captains of the temple." John identifies those who came for Jesus as "a band of soldiers and some officers from the chief priests and the Pharisees." In every Gospel, Judas is said to identify his master with the kiss of betrayal. Those who came to arrest him were armed, as was at least one of Jesus' disciples, whom John identifies as Peter. He defended Jesus, striking one of the high priest's slaves with his sword, severing his ear. Again, John adds a name, identifying the victim as one "Malchus." Luke alone adds the note that Jesus then healed the man. Three of the four Gospels agree that Jesus responded with an emphatic rejection of such violence. Matthew records Jesus' words to this point, "All who take the sword will perish by the sword." Jesus was led away for trial and his disciples did indeed scatter as he had predicted.

Mark alone tells one of the most mysterious stories in all the Gospels when he adds a few cryptic verses about a "young man" who followed Jesus for a while after he was arrested, wearing nothing but a linen cloth. They seized him also, but he slipped from them and fled, naked, leaving the linen cloth behind. Mark may tell us this story to foreshadow Jesus' resurrection, the linen cloth being Jesus' burial shroud, the soldiers death, and the naked young man who escaped them, the Risen Christ.

The Powers That Be

To understand better the events to come—Jesus' trial and execution—it is important to recall the various powers at play in volatile Jerusalem during those tumultuous days.

- The crowds that filled the city during Passover were prominent on two occasions in the story. They greeted Jesus enthusiastically when he entered the city on Palm Sunday. Five days later another crowd gathered before Pontius Pilate near the end of Jesus' trial and called out, "Crucify him!" There is no way to know whether these two crowds contained some of the same individuals, presumably fickle in their affections, or if they were composed of different people. But the "crowd" was always in the background, a volatile ingredient that had to be factored into the decisions of the powerful.

- The Pharisees, religious arch-rivals of Jesus, both in Galilee and during the last few days in Jerusalem, seemed to play little direct role in Jesus' trial and death. In fact, they are barely mentioned in relationship to Jesus' arrest, trial, and execution. John notes that before Palm Sunday they had complained to the council about the attention Jesus was getting from the masses, and later that the "detachment" sent to arrest Jesus was from the "chief priests and the Pharisees."

- The Sadducees, another Jewish religious group, had well-connected priests and was especially committed to the Temple. They are noted only as debating partners during the days before Jesus' arrest and are not mentioned as part of his trial and death. One might assume that many of the "chief priests, elders, and scribes" who did play a central role in his trial were members of this clerical party, however.

- Herod Antipas, tetrarch of Galilee, was one of the sons of Herod the Great to whom the Magi had gone seeking the child born to be King of the Jews more than thirty years earlier. "Tetrarch" was a title that Rome often used to designate vassal provincial rulers in Palestine. This tetrarch was the same Herod who had executed John the Baptist just a few years earlier. This later Herod did not rule in Jerusalem, but seems to have been in the city for the Passover celebration. Luke tells us that after Pilate interviewed Jesus, he sent him to Herod because Jesus was from Galilee and was properly Herod's problem. That night, Herod was at first intrigued with Jesus, but then he and his soldiers mocked him, dressing him in "gorgeous apparel." Herod finally sent him back to Pilate.

- Pontius Pilate was the Roman governor of Judea, appointed by Caesar, in power from 26 to 36. He alone had the authority to sentence a person to death, so it was to Pilate that the local powers sent Jesus for his final trial. Roman governors generally ruled in a close, though often uneasy, alliance with local power elites, in this case the "chief priests and elders of the people."

- The chief priests, elders and scribes represented local religious and political power in Jerusalem and, with Pilate, were central in effecting Jesus' arrest, trial, and execution. Traditionally, seventy-one of them formed the council, or Sanhedrin, which was presided over by a high priest appointed by the Roman governor. At the time of Jesus' trial, one Annas and his son-in-law Caiaphas seem to have been serving overlapping terms as high priest, as Jesus was interrogated by each. Their powerful family was notoriously pro-Roman in sympathy. The council that tried Jesus exercised both religious and political authority. Indeed, power structures at the time, especially among the Jews, made little or no distinction between the religious and the secular.

The question of culpability has long haunted the story of Jesus' death. Who, exactly, was responsible? The issue has been exacerbated by later Christian interpretations that have assigned most or all blame to the Jewish people, leading to the question, Did the Jews kill Jesus? Blaming the Jewish people has often been encouraged by the way the Gospel of John uses a term usually translated as "the Jews" to designate Jesus' foes both during the years of his ministry and the last week of his life.

Several key considerations must be remembered, however. First, the Greek term *hoi Ioudaioi*, traditionally translated as "the Jews", is perhaps better rendered, "the Judeans," meaning those from Jerusalem and

Judea, as opposed to Galilee. John seems to use the term as shorthand for the Jerusalem power elite, not all persons of Jewish faith or birth. Second, except for Pilate, it's essential to remember that everyone in the story is Jewish—Jesus, his disciples, his other supporters, the council, Herod, and the "crowds," both friendly and unfriendly. The story does not pit Jew against non-Jew, but rather unfolds a bitter internal spiritual and political crisis within the Jewish community. Finally, the force of the Gospel accounts of the passion argue for a culpability that is broadly shared, not only by all the players in the historical drama—the council, Pilate, Herod, even Jesus' cowardly disciples—but by all humanity.

Trials

The first stage of Jesus' trial was before the council, or Sanhedrin, those "chief priests and elders of the people," and was presided over by the high priest. Peter had followed the arresting party at a distance, but remained outside in "the courtyard of the high priest" during the first part of the trial. He was recognized while there—it seems his Galilean accent gave him away—and was asked if he was one of Jesus' followers. He denied it three times, then the cock crowed.

Meanwhile, inside, the high priest was prosecuting the case against Jesus on a charge of "blasphemy." Blasphemy was understood to be any gross insult to God (cursing or slandering God) and was punishable by death. Witnesses were called; some were said to lie, others claimed to have heard Jesus say he would destroy the Temple and build another, "not made by hands," in three days. This testimony accurately recalled Jesus' metaphorical reference earlier in the week, comparing the Temple to himself and his impeding death and resurrection. Alarming words, but not blasphemy, the capital offence they were seeking to prove.

At this point in the narratives of the first three Gospels, the high priest asked Jesus point-blank if he were the Messiah; that is, the Christ or Anointed One. Jesus answered that he was. In the minds of his interrogators, this was clearly the blasphemy they were aiming to prove.

But, ironically, only pagan Pilate, the secular authority, could impose a sentence of capital punishment for the religious crime of blasphemy. Before remanding him to Pilate for a second trial the next morning, the council had Jesus mocked and beaten, presumably late in the night or in the darkness of early morning.

At this point in the story, Matthew's Gospel interjects the fate of Judas the betrayer. Judas repented his treachery, attempted to return the thirty pieces of silver that bought his loyalty, and then hung himself. The Book of Acts offers an even grislier end to Judas, who is said to have bought a field with his silver and, "falling headlong, he burst open in the middle."

Friday morning, Jesus was presented by representatives of the council before the Roman governor, Pilate, for his second trial. All the Gospels tell us that Pilate asked Jesus a subtly different question from the one he had been asked the night before. Instead of asking the council's theological question, "Are you the Messiah?" he put a more political query to him, "Are you the King of the Jews?" Jesus answered indirectly but affirmatively, "You have said so." As one might expect, the Roman governor's worries seem to have been less about theological matters and more about the potentially dangerous political pretensions of a person claiming the title "King." There is no way to know whether Pilate was aware of Jesus' nonpolitical use of the term, or if Pilate actually believed him a deluded pretender to political power.

All of the Gospels picture Pilate as reluctant to condemn Jesus to death. Indeed, each includes the story of one Barabbas, a notorious common criminal. According to the Gospels, it was customary during the Passover for the governor to release a condemned man chosen by popular demand. Pilate offered the crowd the choice of Jesus or Barabbas. They cried out for Barabbas' release and for Jesus' death. John's Gospel relates the most extended conversation between Pilate and Jesus, one that ends with Pilate asking, "What is truth?"

As noted earlier, Luke alone includes the story of a third trial of sorts, that before Herod Antipas. Pilate was clearly trying to pawn his problem off on Herod, tetrarch of Galilee, Jesus' home district, who was in the city for the Passover. But after humiliating him, Herod simply sent Jesus back to Pilate. Luke tells us that these two had previously disliked each other, but now began a friendship.

All of the Gospels tell us that Pilate finally condemned Jesus to death, and all but Luke add that that his soldiers then scourged him and mock him. They crowned him with thorns, dressed him in royal purple, put a reed for a scepter in his hand, spat upon him, and knelt before him, calling out, "Hail, King of the Jews." The beating noted in several of the Gospels is never described in detail. In fact, one of the intriguing characteristics of the Gospel accounts of the passion and crucifixion is that in spite of the obviously horrific nature of the events, they are never described in gory detail.

Death

Crucifixion

Crucifixion was a particularly horrific method of execution that had long been widely practiced by different groups in the ancient world. Though they did not invent it, the Romans used it extensively. Ancient historians record any number of mass crucifixions, usually following failed revolutions. Roman citizens and other members of the elite were usually spared crucifixion, leading to the general impression that it was a death fit only for slaves. Thus, the means of Jesus' death was not only painful, but profoundly demeaning.

The word crucifixion comes from two Latin words: *crux*, or cross, and *figere*, "to attach." A victim was bound to two wooden beams, either by nails through the hands and feet, or tied by ropes. The Gospels do not specifically tell us how Jesus was fastened to his cross, but after his resurrection, in two Gospel accounts he showed his hands, implying that they bore some evidence of nail wounds.

Death by crucifixion came from loss of blood or asphyxiation, sometimes in hours, sometimes not for days. Jesus died after several hours. Generally, Roman practice was to leave corpses on their crosses as a warning to other potential malefactors, but in deference to Jewish customs requiring prompt burial, especially during Passover, Jesus' body was almost immediately interred.

It was customary for the condemned person to carry the horizontal beam of his own cross to the site of execution. The first three Gospels all agree that, for unknown reasons, the Roman solders leading Jesus to his execution compelled a passer-by named Simon (doubtless a Jewish pilgrim who is from Cyrene in North Africa) to carry Jesus' cross.

The place of execution was named the Place of the Skull—Golgotha in Aramaic, Calvary in Latin. The time of execution was probably late morning on Friday; the first three Gospels indicate that from noon to three, the hours of his suffering, "there was darkness over the whole land."

All the Gospels tell of the crucifixion with notable reserve, some adding details that others omit. Two of them note that Jesus was first offered wine, perhaps mixed with myrrh, perhaps as a sedative, but that he refused it. All agree that he was crucified between two criminals. Luke, in fact, records the conversation between them and Jesus in which Jesus said to one of them, "Truly, I tell you, today you will be with me in Paradise." All Gospels agree that the solders who executed Jesus gambled for his clothing, implying that when on the cross he was naked, or nearly so. All tell of the inscription on a sign that Pilate had affixed to the cross above Jesus' head reading (in slightly various wordings) "The King of the Jews." John notes that is was inscribed in three languages: Hebrew, Latin, and Greek.

Those present included not only his executioners, but some of his enemies, as well as friends and family. The first three Gospels record bitter taunts directed at Jesus while he was on the cross from "those who pass by" and from "rulers," as well as the soldiers present. Luke tells us that "all his acquaintances" watched the scene from some distance. But all four Gospels agree on one extraordinary point: nearly all of those present out of concern for him were women. Among the four Gospels, seven individuals are specifically identified, six of them women:

> Mary Magdalene,
> Mary, the mother of James and Joseph (or Joses) and probably also wife of Cleopas,
> the unnamed mother of the sons of Zebedee,
> one Salome from Galilee,
> Mary, Jesus' mother,
> and finally, the only male specifically identified –the unnamed "disciple whom he loved,"
> mentioned only in John's Gospel.

The presence of these women initiates a theme that would be echoed twice, at the tomb later that night and two days later at the resurrection—women stood by Jesus when most of the men among his followers did not. This might be explained by the fact that at the scene of the crucifixion women would have presumably been in less danger of arrest than men, and that when the women went to the tomb two days later to anoint his body, they were only doing what was traditionally understood to be women's work. Nevertheless, the central role of women, their faithfulness and later their witness, is jarring in a radically patriarchal culture that dismissed the spirituality of women and their reliability as witnesses.

The four Gospels together (but not one of them alone) record Jesus speaking a total of seven times from the cross, the so-called seven last words. Because they are drawn from four Gospel accounts, it is not possible to establish a definitive sequence in which they might have been uttered. Nevertheless, a review of Jesus' utterances in their traditional order offers another window into the passion story.

>   1. "Father, forgive them, for they do not know what they are doing." (Some ancient versions of Luke record this prayer to God on behalf of his executioners.)

>   2. "Truly, I tell you, you will be with me in Paradise." (Luke records these words as spoken to one of the two criminals crucified with him.)

3. "Woman, here is your son" and "Here is your mother." (John's record of Jesus' words to his mother and the unnamed "disciple whom he loved.")

4. *"Éli, Eli lema sabachthani?"* (Matthew and Mark both recall Jesus' death cry, uttered in Aramaic and meaning "My God, My God, why have you forsaken me." (The words echo Psalm 22 but are misunderstood by some present at the crucifixion who are under the impression that Jesus is calling Elijah to rescue him.)

5. "I am thirsty." (John alone records these words.)

6. "It is finished." (Again from John.)

7. "Father, into your hands I commend my spirit." (The last words of Jesus as recorded by Luke.)

In addition to the hours of darkness noted in several of the Gospels, other cataclysmic phenomena are also recorded at or near the moment of Jesus' death. All of them are meant to underscore the cosmic importance of this particular death. The curtain in the Temple in Jerusalem was torn into two, perhaps a sign of the end of the old order and of access to the new. Matthew records an earthquake, the opening of tombs, and a resurrection of the saints, presumably righteous Jews, all foreshadowing Jesus' resurrection. The first three Gospels all tell the story of a Roman centurion, a minor military officer and presumably one of Jesus' executioners, who upon watching his death declared, "Certainly, this man was innocent!" (Luke) and "Truly, this man was the Son of God!" (Mark and Matthew). Later readers will consider this "confession" a sign of how the larger world of Gentiles would come to recognize the nature of Jesus' identity.

Burial

All four Gospels tell us that when evening came, Jesus' body was interred in a tomb owned by one Joseph of Arimathea, who is variously identified as wealthy, a member of the council, and a secret disciple of Jesus. This Joseph asked Pilate for the body, probably knowing that the usual Roman practice would have been to leave it on the cross for days, if not months.

Joseph of Arimathea had the body wrapped in a linen burial shroud and placed in his tomb, which we are told was "hewn out of the rock." Most tombs of the time were cavelike, cut horizontally into a hillside or cliff, often containing space for more than one body to be laid in niches carved in the walls. The first three Gospels tell us that some of the women among his followers watched the interment, and Luke notes that they then returned home to ready spices and ointments for the body the next day. John tells us that

Nicodemus, a Pharisee whom Jesus had met during his ministry but was now a follower, brought myrrh and aloes to anoint the body. Matthew tells us about a guard posted in front of the tomb so that Jesus' disciples could not steal the body and, declare him raised from the dead.

Life—The Last Word

If the story of Jesus of Nazareth ended with his crucifixion and death, the man and his life would have been
long forgotten. The power that the story of Jesus has
held over billions of people in diverse cultures for the
last two thousand years is not rooted simply in the
profundity of his teaching, in extraordinary miracles, or
in his tragic death come too soon. Jesus was a brilliant
spiritual teacher, but there have been others whose
words captivated the human imagination. Others are
said to have worked miracles that thoroughly mystified
onlookers. And, of course, history has certainly known
more than enough brutal murders of good men and
women.

The sequence of events in Jesus' life as told in the
four Gospels may vary somewhat. Each Gospel
writer tells the story from a distinctive theological
vantage point. One may include an episode like the
story of Jesus' birth that another omits. But the four
draw together and stand shoulder-to-shoulder with

114

each other and with the other books of the New Testament, indeed with veritably every Christian document written in those first centuries, on one emphatic point. All agree that on the third day after his death, Jesus of Nazareth rose from the dead.

All historic witnesses affirm that the resurrection was not precisely something Jesus did *himself*, at least not in the strict sense, but rather something God did to and through him. As an "act of God," the resurrection finally lies beyond human understanding and on the other side of mortal words. Yet the Gospel writers, in stories that are lean and direct, put this mystery into narrative form so that they may faithfully bear witness to the whole reality of Jesus.

The accounts of Jesus' resurrection can be divided into three movements. All of the Gospels include the first two movements; all except the oldest version of Mark's Gospel contain all three. The first movement is the discovery that Jesus' tomb is empty. The second is the encounter with a messenger or messengers (identified as angels in two accounts, a young man in a white robe in another, and two men in dazzling apparel in yet another). But in each case their message is similar: Jesus is not here; he has risen. The third movement, not included in the original edition of Mark, tells of the Risen Christ appearing to his followers.

An Empty Tomb

By all accounts, the original discovery of Jesus' empty tomb was made by several of the women among his followers very early on what was then called the "first day of the week," the day we call Sunday. Two Gospels, Mark and Luke, specifically say that they had gone to the tomb to take care of the preparation of his body for final burial. This anointing of a body was both traditional burial custom and an act of devotion. It seems to have been work usually assigned to women. All four Gospels name one or more of these women. Each includes Mary Magdalene; others add "the other Mary," Mary "the mother of James," Salome, Joanna, and "the other women." In John's Gospel, when the women saw that the stone door had been removed, they returned to tell Peter and "the other disciple, the one whom Jesus loved," who then dashed to the tomb to verify that Jesus' body was indeed gone.

Messengers

An empty tomb is in itself proof of nothing. The body might have been stolen. Indeed, Matthew specifically mentions this possibility and relates a plot by the religious authorities in Jerusalem to start a rumor that the disciples had done just that. All four Gospels tell us that the meaning of the empty tomb—resurrection and not deceit—was presented to the women by a messenger or messengers at the tomb. The words spoken by these messenger(s) vary from Gospel to Gospel. They told the women not to be afraid or not to be amazed. The messenger(s) told them what had happened and that it was precisely what Jesus had promised, but no one understood. Finally, all say that Jesus had indeed risen from the dead. In two of the Gospels the messenger(s) told the women that Jesus was "still in Galilee," or that he was "going before them" into Galilee.

The emotional reaction of the women is described as ranging from joy to terror. In John's Gospel, Mary Magdalene is pictured as distraught at the sight of the empty tomb. John records a gentle and lovely conversation, first with two angels and then with the Risen Christ, that converted Mary's tears to courage. Matthew also tells us that the women encountered the Risen Christ himself, who repeated the injunctions of the angels not to be afraid and to tell the disciples what they had seen, and to go to Galilee.

In what most scholars think is the original, shorter ending of Mark's Gospel, the women are said to have been so terrified that they said nothing about what they had seen. The other Gospels continue the story and indicate that the women themselves became messengers who related what they had seen and heard to their fellow male disciples, who were still hiding. Both Luke and John indicate that the men reacted with skepticism. Indeed, Luke says, "These words seemed to them an idle tale and they did not believe them."

In a world that did not permit women to bear testimony in court, the fact that women are universally named as the first witnesses to the resurrection is yet another instance of the reversal of the conventional understanding of truth and power.

Appearances

Save for the blunt original version of Mark that ends

with the women at the tomb frightened and unable to say anything of what they had seen, the Gospels all conclude with the stories of several manifestations of the Risen Christ to his disciples. Matthew tells of the appearance of Jesus to his eleven disciples on a mountaintop in Galilee to which they had gone. His words to them include the commandment to "make disciples of all nations, baptizing them in the name of the Father and of the Son and of the Holy Spirit." These words are traditionally called the Great Commission; it is one of the few times in the Bible where the Trinity is explicitly named.

Luke centers his telling of the appearance of the Risen Christ in a subtle and longer tale about two disciples (including one not previously mentioned named Cleopas) who were walking to a village not far from Jerusalem named Emmaus, on the Sunday of the resurrection.

A stranger took up the journey with them and together they spoke of the events of the last few days— the death of Jesus and the story of his resurrection. The stranger, in words we are not told, interpreted the meaning of these events to the two disciples. They implored him to have dinner with them in Emmaus, even though he "appeared to be going further." The stranger joined them at table, and when he broke bread with them, "their eyes were opened and they recognized him."

They returned to Jerusalem and told the others that they had encountered the Risen Christ. Suddenly, Jesus stood among all of them. He showed them his hands and feet as testimony that it was indeed he who had been crucified. He ate, again a way of demonstrating life, and, most important, he "opened their minds to understand the scriptures." He finally commissioned them to bear witness about him to "all nations," then led them out of the city as far as Bethany, where he blessed them and parted from them. In the opening chapter of his second book, Acts, Luke adds more details about this parting, traditionally called the Ascension.

The appearances of the Risen Christ in the last chapter of John's Gospel include several incidents that most scholars believe were added in later editions of the book. In what is probably the older version, John ends with Jesus coming twice to his disciples while they were in a locked room in Jerusalem. In the first of these two encounters, Jesus symbolically breathed upon them, giving them the gift of the Holy Spirit. The second encounter, set a week later, centered around Thomas. This "doubting Thomas," as tradition has named him, was a disciple who had not been present a week earlier and had declared that he would not believe secondhand reports of resurrection, but must see for himself. Thomas saw and believed. Last, the Risen Christ spoke words crucial to those who would read John's Gospel a half century later, words equally powerful for all who would encounter Jesus throughout the ages: "Blessed are those who have not seen, and yet believe."

Why Should Anyone Care?

There are at least three good answers to the question of why anyone should care about a Galilean rabbi who lived two thousand years ago. The first answer is "intellectual curiosity." The second answer is "spiritual curiosity," and the third answer is the traditional response of Christian believers, among whom I count myself.

Intellectual Curiosity

Even people who make no pretense of being followers of Jesus often have a keen interest in knowing his story, simply because it's important for any well-informed person to know about a life that has had such a seminal impact on history. In much the same way, a well-read capitalist might want to know something about the thought of Karl Marx, a Jew might want to read the Muslim Quran, or a Christian might study the life of Confucius.

We live in a world in which different religions and

cultures intersect in unprecedented ways. The communications and transportation revolutions, mass migration, and international travel mean that religions that once lived in isolation now meet each other daily on the street and on television screens. And contrary to expectations of many, religion is not playing a decreasing role in human history. Rather, the importance of faith in many cultures in the world is clearly in ascendancy. Christianity, the faith of those who follow Jesus, is the largest single religion in the world. Put simply, more people on earth identify themselves in some way with Jesus Christ than any other person, faith, or philosophy in history, and whether or not you count yourself among them, it's obviously important to know the story of the most influential individual of all time.

Spiritual Curiosity

Our world is witnessing a burgeoning interest in spirituality. In spite of material prosperity and personal success, many people long for deeper meaning and transcendent purpose in their lives. In the face of death and the other mysteries of mortal existence, people long for a framework that makes some sense of it all. This spiritual thirst has led to a renewed interest in traditional and nontraditional spiritual teachers, Jesus among them. Indeed, the teachings of Jesus continue to influence many men and women who would not call themselves Christians.

Such searchers often encounter much in the story of Jesus that they find helpful, comforting, and challenging. But some are tempted to read the story of

121

Jesus very selectively. They sometimes are inclined to cherry-pick the teachings of Jesus, plucking those that resonate with them personally and ignoring those that do not. They revel in the parts of his story that appeal to them, while editing out portions they find baffling or offensive.

Often the Jesus of such selectivity is Jesus the kindly rabbi who took children onto his knees, or the Jesus of the Sermon on the Mount (or at least portions of it), or the Jesus who told the parable of the Good Samaritan. But often edited out of this personally popular Jesus is the Jesus who performed miracles that stymie the modern mind. Neatly omitted is the Jesus who castigated Pharisees for hypocrisy. Edited out is the Jesus who issued discomfortingly radical calls for all-or-nothing discipleship. Such a way of reading the story of Jesus often skims over the dramatic claims Jesus made about himself in the Gospels, claims that clearly indicate that he understood himself to be more than just a wise teacher of love, compassion, and spiritual values. But the part of the story most often omitted in such selective versions of Jesus is the end—that brutal, scandalous, ineffable, and mystifying tale of passion, death, and resurrection.

Perhaps the greatest problem with an "edited Jesus," however, is that Jesus himself—in his teachings and in his actions—seemed to discourage a take-it-as-you-like-it approach. For instance, he clearly understood himself to be more than just a teacher. His call to those who might follow him was uncompromising. His miracles were not extraneous oddities that can be snipped out of the story by those discomforted by mystery. And, like it or not, Jesus' whole life pointed toward that last week with its scandalous cross and inexplicable resurrection. These final events were no mere awkward epilogue; they were the climax that defined his life.

Historic Christianity

The traditional Christian response has been to receive the whole story of Jesus, the comforting and the discomforting, the clear and the baffling, the easy and the demanding alike. In doing so, the historic Christian understanding of who Jesus was, what he did, and what it all means emerged in the years following his life when Christians reflected back on his story. The following observations offer but the briefest sketch of this historic Christian understanding of Jesus.

First, the traditional Christian understanding of Jesus affirms that he was—as he himself claimed and as the Gospels claim of him—the One awaited by the prophets of the Old Testament; that is, the Anointed One, the Messiah, or the Christ. As such, he is named Jesus Christ. He is also named Son of God, meaning not only "one close to God" in a general sense, but the One who is close to God in unique way. So profoundly close to God that Christians confess him to be "divine," indeed, to *be* God. Remember, of course, that all such language about God treads the ragged edge of human ability to speak of matters that are ultimately outside our full comprehension.

Second, because of who Jesus is, the Christian understanding is that what he said is uniquely authoritative. Jesus was a teacher, but not just another teacher. His teaching is understood as part of the ancient Jewish tradition of spiritual wisdom, but Jesus' word is received as the definitive interpretation of that wisdom. This is not to say that Jesus' teachings negate or supersede all others. But his word is heard not just as one word among many, but as a word from God. As such, Jesus' call to love others selflessly, to love God totally, and to offer compassion and forgiveness generously are at the nonnegotiable core of Christianity. Such a unique authority leads Christians to call Jesus "Lord."

Third, the Christian faith has historically understood that God "spoke" through Jesus, not just in the words Jesus said, but in and through the way Jesus lived his life. So the manner of Jesus' life—his compassionate healing of the sick, his scandalous welcoming of outcasts and sinners, his utter impatience with hypocrisy, his readiness to give himself totally for others—is understood as an image, drawn in human terms, of the very nature of God. In this way, historic Christianity has understood that Jesus "reveals" God. Of course, by definition God is beyond human understanding, yet the traditional Christian understanding of Jesus is that he is God "incarnate," meaning God "in the flesh"; that is, God offered to us in the only language we can really understand: the "language" of a human life like our own.

Fourth, historic Christianity has understood the passion, death, and resurrection to be the definitive story of how God loves the world. A famous verse in the Gospel of John says it plainly: "For God so loved the

124

world that he gave his only Son." The suffering and death of Jesus demonstrate the depth of the Divine love for humanity. The passion and the cross declare that God is with people not only in the joys of life, but also in the agony and loss that life can bring. And the cross comes to be understood as somehow reconciling the estrangement between God and humanity. Such an understanding would lead historic Christianity to call Jesus not just "Lord," but "Savior." The last word of the story of Jesus is not suffering and death. The last, ultimate and declarative word is "life." In the years that followed Jesus, the greatest day of the Christian calendar would not be Good Friday, but Easter with its uncompromising declaration that God, more than anything, is the God of Life.

Finally and perhaps most crucially, historic Christianity has not simply understood Jesus to be the founder of the Christian faith, but a continuing, living presence in the world and in individual lives. The resurrection not only affirms the triumph of life, it also promises that Jesus is more than a dead memory. He is the ongoing and vital presence of God in life and history. Thus, historic Christianity does not believe the story of Jesus to be completed. Rather, it dares to believe that God in Jesus continues to live and to act, especially through those who follow him as they struggle—sometimes successfully and sometimes unsuccessfully—to live as he lived, to love as he loved, and to give of themselves as he gave of himself.

The Parables of Jesus

Parables Only in Matthew

The Weeds Among the Wheat—Good and evil grow side-by-side in this life. Matthew 13:21-30

The Hidden Treasure—The Gospel is invaluable. Matthew 13:44

The Pearl of Great Value—The Gospel is worth more than anything. Matthew 13:45–47

The Dragnet—The earthly church includes the good and the bad. Matthew 13:47–48

The Unmerciful Servant—Being forgiven requires us to forgive. Matthew 18: 23–34

The Workers in the Vineyard—God is beyond human ideas of fairness. Matthew 20:1–16

The Father and Two Sons—What you actually do is more important than what you say you will do. Matthew 21:28–32

The Wedding of the King's Son's—The most unlikely people accept God's invitation. Matthew 22:1–14

The Wise and Foolish Bridesmaids—Some people are ready; some are not. Matthew 25:1–13

The Talents—Use your gifts for good.
Matthew 25: 14–30

The Sheep and the Goats—Mercy and compassion are what really matter in the end. Matthew 25:31–46

Parables Only in Mark

The Seed Growing in Secret—Faith grows by a mystery we don't understand. Mark 4:26–29

The Doorkeeper—Be watchful. Mark 13:34–36

Parables Only in Luke

The Two Debtors—God's grace is big enough for any sinner. Luke 7:41–50

The Good Samaritan—Unlikely people sometimes do the right thing. Luke 10:30–37

The Friend at Midnight—Don't give up on prayer. Luke 11:5–8

The Rich Fool—You can't store what really matters in a barn. Luke 12:16–21

The Waiting Servant—Be alert. Luke 12:35–40

The Wise and Faithful Servant—Trust demands responsibility. Luke 12:42–48

The Barren Fig Tree—God gives second chances. Luke 13:6–9

The Great Banquet—God invites absolutely everybody to the feast. Luke 14:16–24

The Tower and the Warring King—Count the cost before you follow Jesus. Luke 14:28–33

The Lost Coin—God loves each of us infinitely.
Luke 15:8–10

The Prodigal Son and His Older Brother—God's grace is wide, and ours should be, too. Luke 15:11–32

The Dishonest Manager—Do the best you can in difficult circumstances. Luke 16:1–8

The Rich Man and Lazarus—Wealth absolutely demands generosity. Luke 16:19–31

The Farmer and His Servant—Duty to God ought to be natural. Luke 17:7–10

The Dishonest Judge—If you can get through to him you can surely get through to God. Luke 18:1–8

The Pharisee and the Tax Collector—Humility compared to self–righteousness. Luke 18:9–14

The Parable of the Pounds—Diligence will be rewarded. Luke 19: 12–27

Parable–like Passages Only in John

The Bread of Life—Jesus nourishes our souls.
John 6:25–59

The Shepherd and the Sheep—Jesus is like a shepherd to his followers. John 10:1–39

The Vine and the Branches—Jesus is the vine and his followers are like branches. John 15:1–27

Parables in Two of the Gospels

Houses Built on Rock and Sand—Build you life on the firm foundation. Matthew 7:24–27; Luke 6:48–49

The Leaven—A little of God's truth is powerful.
Matthew 13:33; Luke 13:20–21

The Lost Sheep—God's joy over finding one lost soul.
Matthew 18:12–14; Luke 15:4–7

Parables in Three of the Gospels

The Lamp under the Bushel Basket—Don't hide the light of
God's truth.
Matthew 5:14–16; Mark 4:21–23; Luke 8:16–18

New Cloth on the Old Garment; New wine in Old
Wineskins—New faith might not work on old forms.
Matthew 9:16–17; Mark 2: 21–22; Luke 5:36–39

The Sower—Sometimes people get God's message, sometimes
they don't. Matthew 13:18–30; Mark 4:3–9; Luke 8:5–8

The Mustard Seed—It only takes a little faith.
Matthew 13:31–32; Mark 4:31–32; Luke 13:18–19

The Tenants in the Vineyard—The world often rejects God's
messenger. Matthew 21:33–41; Mark 12:1–8; Luke 21:9–16

New Leaves on the fig Tree—Watch for signs of what's
coming.
Matthew 24:32; Mark 13:38; Luke 21:29–30

The Miracles of Jesus

Miracles Only in Matthew

Two blind men healed – Matthew 9:27–31
A mute demoniac healed—Matthew 9:32–33
A coin found in a fish's mouth—Matthew 17:24–27

Miracles Only in Mark

A deaf mute healed—Mark 7:31–37
A blind man healed—Mark 8:22–26

Miracles Only in Luke

Jesus passes unseen—Luke 4:28–30
The great catch of fish—Luke 5:1–11
The widow's son raised—Luke 7:11–15
A handicapped woman healed—Luke 13:11–13
A man with dropsy healed—Luke 14:1–4
Ten lepers healed—Luke 17:11–19
Malchus' ear healed—Luke 22:50–51

Miracles Only in John

Water changed to wine—John 2:1–11
Official's son healed—John 4:46–54
Invalid at the pool in Jerusalem healed—John 5:1–9
Man born blind healed—John 9:1–7
Lazarus raised—John 11:38–44
The catch of 153 fish—John 21:1–14

Miracles in Two Gospels

Centurion's servant healed
Matthew 8:5–13; Luke 7:1–10

The blind and mute demoniac healed
Matthew 12:22 and Luke 11:14

The Syrophoenician woman's daughter healed
Matthew 15:21–28; Mark 7:24–30

The four thousand fed
Matthew 15:32–38; Mark 8:1–9

The fig tree cursed—Matthew 21:19; Mark 11:14

The demoniac in the synagogue healed
Mark 1:23–26; Luke 4:33–35

Miracles in Three Gospels

The leper healed—Matthew 8:2–3; Mark 1:40–41, Luke
5:12–13

Peter's mother–in–law healed—Matthew 8:14–15; Mark
1:30–31; Luke 4:38–39

The storm stilled—Matthew 8:23–26; Mark 4:35–39; Luke
8:22–24

Demons cast into the swine—Matthew 8:28–32, Mark 5:1–13;
Luke 8:26–33

The paralytic healed—Matthew 9:2–7; Mark 2:3–12; Luke
5:18–25

Jairus' daughter raised—Matthew 9:18–26; Mark 5:22–42;
Luke 8:41–56

Woman with a hemorrhage healed—Matthew 9:20–22; Mark
5:25–29; Luke 8:43–48

A man's withered hand healed—Matthew 12:10–13; Mark
3:1–5; Luke 6:6–11

Jesus walks on the water—Matthew 14:25–27; Mark 6:48–51; John 6:19–20

An epileptic boy healed—Matthew 17:14–18; Mark 9:17–27; Luke 9:37–42

Blind man (men) healed—Matthew 20:30–34; Mark 10:46–52; Luke 18:35–43

Miracle in Four Gospels

The feeding of the five thousand—Matthew 14:15–21; Mark 6:35–44; Luke 9:10–17, John 6:1–14

Michael L. Lindvall is an author and minister, presently serving as the senior minister of the Brick Church in New York City. He has written two novels, *The Good News from North Haven* and *Leaving North Haven*, as well as a volume of accessible theology, *A Geography of God*, to be released in 2006. He is married to Terri Vaun Smith, an artist, teacher, and homemaker. The Lindvalls make their home in Manhattan.